OLD HOUSE COLORS

An Expert's Guide to Painting Your Old (Or Not So Old) House

Lawrence Schwin III

A Sterling/Main Street Book
Sterling Publishing Co., Inc.   New York

Designed by Ronald R. Misiur

Library of Congress Cataloging-in-Publication Data
Schwin, Lawrence.
  Old house colors: an expert's guide to painting your old (or not so old) house /
Lawrence Schwin III.
    p. cm.
    "A Sterling/Main Street book."
    Includes bibliographical references.
    1. House painting. 2 Color. I. Title.
TT320.S38 1990
698'. 12—dc20

                                                    90-36971
                                                    CIP

10 9 8 7 6 5 4 3 2 1

A Sterling / Main Street Book

Text © 1990 by Lawrence Schwin III
Illustrations © 1990 by Sterling Publishing Company, Inc.
Published by Sterling Publishing Company, Inc.,
387 Park Avenue South, New York, N.Y. 10016.
Distributed in Canada by Sterling Publishing,
c/o Canadian Manda Group, P.O. Box 920, Station U,
Toronto, Ontario, Canada M8Z 5P9.
Distributed in Great Britain and Europe by Cassell PLC,
Villiers House, 41/47 Strand, London WC2N 5JE. England.
Distributed in Australia by Capricorn Ltd.,
P.O. Box 665, Lane Cove, NSW 2066.
Printed in Hong Kong

Sterling ISBN 0-8069-7430-3

Contents

AS INTEREST IN historic preservation has grown and matured in the United States during the past two decades, more precise information concerning furnishings, architectural developments, and cultural life has deepened our feeling for the past. Increasingly, complex and sophisticated scientific investigations have revealed more accurate pictures of our architectural patrimony. Not the least of these discoveries has been that concerned with historic paint research, a discipline which is revealing surprising and even startling clues about the painted environments of our American ancestors.

The studies which comprise the text of this book are indicative of the growing interest in authentic color and its use on building exteriors from the early eighteenth century through the first few decades of the twentieth. Arranged roughly chronologically to encompass each of the major architectural styles, color selections are shown on elevations of actual period buildings, each of which is from the extraordinary Historic American Buildings Survey collection (HABS) housed at the Library of Congress. Recorded by architects and students since the 1930s, this collection chronicles the history of America's built environment. The houses illustrated were selected with a number of criteria in mind, including their ability to illustrate color selections, geographic location, and the architectural qualities of the buildings themselves. While only two of the houses illustrated are among the country's finest domestic examples—the John N. A. Griswold House and the Vernon House, both in Newport, Rhode Island—the remainder are good and commonly seen examples of American domestic building.

In looking at the HABS drawings, it is important to remember that many of them record a structure's condition at the time of investigation. Many, therefore, show architectural additions which date from a period well after initial construction. Elements as simple as the nineteenth-century shutters on the eighteenth-century Vernon House (chapter 3) and the Italianate-style side porch of Georgian-style Harmony Hall (chapter 6) exemplify this situation. In these instances, elements which are not necessarily of the period of initial construction have been left on the illustrations, in part to illustrate how minor additions might be handled

Preface

by the homeowner in similar situations. In other examples, major modern intrusions such as dormer windows or sliding glass doors have been eliminated as indeed they might be on actual examples being restored. In still other examples, features which appear to have been lost over time have been "restored" in order to present a more realistic architectural portrait of the building type being illustrated. The balustrade at the roof of the David Alling House (Chapter 12) and the chimney pots on the stacks of the J. Mora Moss House (Chapter 20) are examples of this "restorative license." In all instances, however, the houses pictured have been used as a means of illustrating colors appropriate to the architectural styles which they represent.

Old House Colors, as the title implies, is primarily interested in assisting the owner of a period house in the selection of a color scheme appropriate to the period and style of its construction. Beyond that, the book will also be useful to those homeowners whose houses may not be old but which are stylistic adaptations of many of the buildings illustrated. To this end, each of the thirty-five drawings has been colored with one appropriate color scheme, listed as scheme A in the chart accompanying each illustration. Two additional schemes, labeled B and C, have also been included in each chart. Additional information has also been provided, where applicable, in the notes section for each chapter. In each instance, the names of commercially available paints which most closely approximate historic colors are listed. The notation for "body," for example, refers to the major house color. Paint schemes for masonry and stucco-covered houses have also been included since the colors chosen for stucco and those used on trim, doors, and shutters of brick and stone houses are important considerations. Recognizing that paint names change and that companies periodically discontinue certain colors, each color listed in the text has been listed in an appendix along with a Munsell color notation number. The Munsell system, a universal classification system for color, will enable anyone to match the color name specified with an unchanging color reference.

Since architectural styles and cultural ideas have been a strong determining factor in American paint history, the text accompanying each illustration provides information pertinent to the selection of the color schemes. One clear thread which runs throughout our paint heritage is the fact that the colors often chosen for the exteriors of buildings, and especially those used on domestic structures, seem to comprise somewhat of a social science in itself. This was especially clear by the 1830s when, for example, colors were influenced not only by architectural styles but also by the philosophical ideas concerning the use of certain colors within the landscape. As the century progressed, these aspects were augmented by the development of more sophisticated paint technologies and the availability of ready-mixed paints.

My research for the study which follows has been guided and necessarily influenced by a background in cultural history, historic preservation, and architecture. A long interest in genre paintings and drawings of American buildings and their interiors, as well as contemporary descriptions of them, formed the beginning of my research for *Old House Colors*. Clearly, the amount of information available is large and, happily, surprisingly consistent. In addition, the reported findings of historic paint researchers and the subsequent re-painting in authentic fashion of many historic buildings across the country have made this study significantly easier than it would have been even five years ago. It is especially noteworthy, as well, that several major American restorations, long revered for their accurate portrayal of the American past, have begun to re-color both the interior and exteriors of their buildings to more closely mirror early or original paint schemes. Indeed, it seems likely, given some of the discoveries made during the past

few years, that Americans interested in a more accurate color picture of our past will have to become accustomed to some unique and even startling colors. Even as the "authentic" Colonial colors of the last half-century have influenced our own color sensibilities, it is tempting to speculate that the new colors, discovered by chemical and light-microscopy methods will do the same for the next generation.

I ONCE HEARD it said that nothing of any real effort in life is ever a solitary act, a sentiment that often came to mind during the production of *Old House Colors*. Without the help of several people, this book would never have become a reality. I acknowledge with thanks my friend Susan Gallagher, who suggested that I write the book, and those teachers and colleagues who, over twenty years, have encouraged my interest in American architecture and design—Dr. J. Stanley Mattson; James R. Short; Charles H. Detwiller, Jr., AIA; Gordon B. Varey, AIA; John I. Pearce, AIA; and J. Robert Hillier, FAIA. I thank, too, my editors at The Main Street Press, Lawrence Grow and Martin Greif, and Dr. Robert S. Miner, Jr., a good family friend and consulting chemist, who reviewed the chemical information in this book. My parents, who have supported me in many ways, have cultivated my lifelong interest in preservation, a loving act for which I cannot thank them enough. Finally, I thank my sister Joan for providing me with food and shelter and good company during my research at the Library of Congress. There, Mary Ison, head reference librarian, Prints and Photographs Division, offered invaluable assistance in locating archival material.

THROUGHOUT MOST of our history, the task of house painting was considered a craft; that is, a highly skilled procedure that required a system of apprenticeship leading to a master's ability.[1] Apparently, house painting was often allied to other manners of decorative painting. Among these were the painting of shop signs, floorcloths, and even ships. Richard Candee, a well-known scholar of early American life, recently noted at a national conference concerning historic paint colors that painters often had to develop skills to enable them to paint in imitation of fabricated materials such as copperplating, lead, and even calicos in interior areas where, for example, a wooden valance might come into contact with cloth![2] We know, as well, that throughout the eighteenth century and well into the nineteenth painters had to be well adept at marbleization, the imitation of wood graining, and the preparation of stuccoed or plastered surfaces to appear as stone blocking. Indicative of the wide variety of the painting craft are words by an early nineteenth-century American painter written to acquaint the public with the task of painting. In a book written in 1812 and entitled *Directions for House and Ship Painting; Shewing . . . the Best Method of Preparing, Mixing and Laying the Various Colors now in Use, Designed for the Use of Learners,* Hezekiah Reynolds noted that his directions were designed to appeal to "the Cabinet and Chair maker, the Wheelwright, the House and Ship-Joiner and to others whose trades are connected with building."[3]

While the colors used by the American painter have generally reflected the prevalent taste of the specific period, varieties of pigments were available throughout most of the eighteenth century. Despite the current belief that buttermilk paints were widely used for exteriors in the past, most of the painted houses were actually given applications of oil-based paints which were generally comprised of linseed oil, white lead, and a pigment admixture. Milk-based paints, concoctions of milk and color agents, were far less stable than oil-based paints and apparently had little practical use after the invention of the former in the fifteenth century.[4] Whitewashes, however, which were popular on interior as well as some exterior surfaces, were, as one scholar has noted, "A kind of liquid plaster."[5] Chemically known as calcium carbonate,

Introduction

whitewash is composed of an interlocking crystaline structure which binds to itself, unlike paint which depends on a binding agent. Used primarily on outbuildings and sheds, it was an inexpensive alternative to paint and was simply a mixture of lime and water which absorbed carbon dioxide from the atmosphere.

The most common method of mixing color for exterior use was to grind one's own pigment and then add it to white lead in its dry form before mixing with oil. Not surprisingly, this procedure was potentially hazardous since lead and some of the pigments used were very toxic. A condition known as "painter's colic" or *Colica pictonum* was a progressive disease brought about by the improper handling of lead and other toxic pigments such as those containing mercury, arsenic, and verdigris. One writer likened the debilitating effects of the disease to those of "a paralyzed walking mummy."[6]

Most paint historians seem to agree that between 1750 and 1850 the craft of painting remained virtually unchanged.[7] Though ready-mixed paints were available during the eighteenth century in a paste-like form, most painters apparently preferred to mix their own colors and paints.[8] This procedure, of course, guaranteed a great deal more control over the color and stressed pride in the craft procedure. While some native materials were employed as coloring agents, most of the pigments in use were reportedly imported during the eighteenth century. Among the most popular and useful for exterior work were white and various reds, yellows, and even blues.[9] White, such as that called "white lead," was characterized by a special brightness. Not only popular as a base color, it also saw a wide use as a primer, a putty, and as a finishing color.

That white lead (lead acetate) was a fairly stable color is partly responsible for its popularity.[10] It was also a relatively easy pigment to make, and most painters apparently continued to do so even after commercial fabrication began in Philadelphia in 1804.[11] A common recipe advised painters to:

> . . . get an earthen vessel with a cover on it, and an earthen colander, with bars instead of holes, made to fit the vessel; the colander should go about half way down; then pour vinegar into the vessel till it nearly reaches the bars of the colander. On the colander place narrow slips of thin lead rolled up into scrolls, these may be placed all over the bars of the colander, taking care that they do not touch each other. The pot is then placed over a gentle heat and the fumes of the vinegar corroding the lead reduces it to a white calx ready for use.[12]

The other favored colors—red, yellow, and blue—were either mixed into white lead or used alone with oils. Red pigments were generally quite stable, very plentiful, and varied, which accounts for their great popularity.[13] One such pigment, called Spanish brown, was a popular primer and was derived by simply separating it "from the stones and filth that were dug up with it," and then ground well in the typical fashion using a muller to grind the fragments against a slab.[14] Yellows, which were equally popular, were either earth-derived or lead derivatives. One variety, which was said to produce a "beautiful golden yellow," was achieved by grinding gallstones or "concretions of earthly matter and bile that were removed from the gall bladders of beasts."[15] Blue pigments, though somewhat scarce, were sometimes derived from ferric ferro-cyanide and were quite popular in America.[16]

After the middle of the nineteenth century hand-mixed paints began to yield gradually to ready-mixed varieties, although one scholar has noted that the craft of mixing pigments into oil by hand did persist to some degree into the first years of the twentieth century.[17] One of the country's first ready-mixed paint collections was fabricated by F. W. Devoe and Company. Developed during the late 1860s, this collection of muted tones in yellows, browns, and russets was presented on what may well have been the first commercial paint card used in America.[18] Consistent with the colors advocated by A. J. Downing* and others as those most con-

---

*Because of the pervasive influence of the theories and writings of Andrew Jackson Downing (1815-1852), it will serve us well to introduce him and his work at the outset of this book. It is, in fact, an understatement to say that his theories, which encompassed landscape planning, architecture, and house colors, among other things, had a great impact on the minds of Americans from the mid-nineteenth century into the first few decades of the twentieth.

Downing was not an architect, although he is often confused with having been one since he is most popularly known for his collaboration with Alexander Jackson Davis (1803-1892) who was one of the best known architects of the nineteenth century. Downing was, instead, a prosperous nurseryman and a publisher whose books, in combination with his talent and engaging personality, assisted in disseminating his ideas and theories. His first book, *A Treatise on the Theory and Practice of Landscape Gardening Adapted to North America* (1841), brought him, through several editions, his initial fame. *Cottage Residences,* which first appeared in 1842 and presented the designs of several architects, also discussed the appropriate colors for the house. The book provided a hand-colored plate, at least in its earliest editions, of six appropriate colors which were said to be "highly suitable for the exterior of cottages and villas." Three shades of gray and three of fawn were depicted and considered ". . . pleasing and harmonious in any situation in the country." Like others of his books, *Cottage Residences* continued to be reprinted decades after his death.

The Architecture of Country Houses (1850), the last of Downing's books, was as popular as its predecessors. Relying heavily on the architectural designs of A. J. Davis, Downing continued to develop, in this work, his ideas of an integration between architecture and the natural setting. Not surprisingly, the work of Davis, which by this time was concentrated in the highly romantic Gothic mode, complemented Downing's ideas of naturalistic and less formalized landscaping. Colors found in nature were felt to be those most suitable to an architecture which, even stylistically, was integrated with its setting. Sounding prophetic, Downing had earlier written:

> The color of buildings may properly be made to increase their expression of truthfulness . . . . There is one color, however, . . . which we feel bound to protest against most heartily . . . . This is white which is so universally applied to our houses of every size and description. The glaring nature of this color, when seen in contrast with the soft green of foliage, renders it extremely unpleasant . . . . To render the effect still worse, our modern builders paint their . . . shutters a bright green! A cool dark green would be in better taste . . . .

Others, perhaps wishing to jump onto Downing's bandwagon or who were themselves convinced of his ideas, produced books of similar character and intent. However, none ever surpassed those produced by Downing nor influenced American design and color theory in quite the same manner.

sistent with the natural landscape, they were, nonetheless, a bit darker and richer than the drabs and taupes of twenty years before.[19] By the 1870s and 1880s, a revolution in exterior color was raging; it was one which reflected not only the deepened color palette but a much more diverse variety of colors from which to choose.[20] However, as Roger Moss and Gail Winkler have noted, the color changes from the muted, naturally-derived colors of Downing gave way only gradually to the rich colors commonly associated with the last decades of the nineteenth century.[21]

Beginning with the Centennial in 1876, American domestic architecture began a gradual movement back to an eighteenth-century inspiration. By the turn of the century, the Colonial Revival style was in full sway, along with an exterior color palette thought to be at least evocative of those used on eighteenth-century houses. The rich colors of the 1880s and '90s were replaced by the yellows, grays, and ever popular white, and it seemed especially true that the old adage about history repeating itself was never truer.

While much of the information about eighteenth-century color, and indeed of all historic color application, has been derived largely in the recent past from paint scraping, modern technologies developed during the past decade or two are revolutionizing our knowledge and conceptions of historic color. Whereas scraped colors often yield unreliable results effected by fading, wear, and the impregnation of dust and dirt as well as pigment discoloration, the highly developed chemical and polarized light microscope analyses being carried out today are uncovering palettes of amazing and, in some instances, even jarring colors.[22] Indeed, it seems logical to believe that we can look forward to an even greater color understanding of our architectural past.

AN UNDERSTANDING OF the authentic color palette of any era and its use on the domestic structures of today is, of course, open to wide varieties of interpretation. The steps which follow are intended to be a guide towards the selection of an appropriate color scheme for use on a period building. Many older houses are today being painted in color pastiches that have little if anything to do with either the color theory or color placement current at the time of the building's construction or with its architectural style and detailing. The following recommendations, used in conjunction with the information provided in the thirty-five drawings and text accompanying them, should enable anyone to select an appropriate historic color scheme for an old (or not so old) house which will also be personally satisfying.

1. Determine the age and style of the house and find out what colors are appropriate to its period. If the house is a newer one styled after the design of an earlier period, follow the recommendations for painting buildings constructed during that period.

2. If the house is a true old one, decide whether or not it should be returned to a color scheme that it may have had at one point in its history. Unless the building has particular historic or architectural interest, reproducing an historic scheme may not be necessary, however desirable. An earlier color scheme may or may not suit the present owner's taste.

3. Determine what kind of preparation and finishes will be compatible with existing painted surfaces. Slapping another coat of paint onto an old house may not be the wisest choice. The removal of existing finishes may be advisable. If so, *extreme care* and the advice of experts is warranted. If paint is to be removed, preserve a record sample of all painted surfaces in some inconspicuous place on the house for future owners. It is possible that someone a century from now may want to paint the house the color it was in the 1990s.

4. Gather a number of paint charts *before* preparing any color schematic drawings since commercial paints are those easiest and least expensive to use. Commercial paint companies produce hundreds of colors closely related to historic ones. Do not assume, however, that a paint color is "historic" merely because the paint company says it is. Compare chips with other chips and with any historic documents available.

Cut out the chips selected and arrange them to determine if the tones and values of the ensemble will work together. The best light for doing this is a north light where glare and bright sun will not distort the effect.

5. Prepare colored schematic drawings on paper before purchasing paint. If there is an architectural elevation drawing of the house available, this can be simply traced onto a sheet of white paper. Run off a number of copies of the image on a photocopier. If the architectural image is too large, it can be reduced to an 8½″ x 11″ sheet on most machines. A good black and white photograph can also be useful.

Colored pencils are best to work up color schemes, and both Berol Prismacolors and Cumberland Derwents—available at art supply stores—are useful. They should be kept sharpened and applied heavily to achieve the best colors. Prismacolors can be applied over Derwent colors to produce color gradations, but not vice versa since Prismacolors are waxier than the Derwents.

Render all windows realistically, that is as black or dark gray so that mullion color selections will read correctly. In *Old House Colors,* windows have been shown with ecru-colored shades as well.

6. After at least two schemes have been prepared, pin them up and study them for several days. The value of this should not be underestimated, for it will prevent hasty decisions. If time allows, a little more research may be needed.

7. If still unsure of a selection, purchase small amounts of the colors thought best and apply them to a portion of the house. The cost of this, compared with the larger cost advantage of buying gallons of paint, is obvious. Apply the colors where they will best show what the overall effect will be. Include the body color, sash, trim, and shutter colors. If the color for the door is important, include that as well.

Most historic paint experts and, indeed, common sense, suggest that storm windows and screens should be painted to match the color chosen for the window sash. A storm or screen door should match the darkest color of the door to which it is affixed. This rule should be followed whether the windows and doors are wood or of a modern metal.

8. Finally, paint the house with the confidence that a good and responsible job has been done in selecting appropriate colors. At the same time, keep in mind the thought that the scheme chosen can be always changed in the future.

BEGINNING A STUDY OF the painted house in America with an example of a brick building may seem unusual, but not when one considers the fact that masonry structures—which form a considerable body of American building—are as dependent upon painted trimwork as their wooden counterparts. In fact, color selection for wooden cornices, framed casings, sash, shutters, doors, and other features demands more careful consideration than that required for framed structures since the color of masonry units is unchangeable and provides the basis upon which secondary color selections are likely to be based.

Recent research indicates that at various times throughout American building history, masonry structures were sometimes painted. The elegant brick façade of Charleston's Miles Brewton House (c. 1769), for example, was reportedly covered with a red wash sometime during the 1700s.[1] Research has suggested, as well, that even the grand façade of William Byrd's Westover Plantation house (c. 1729-35) was similarly painted, and that its fine–gauged brick belt course, laid in Flemish bond, was painted white.[2] To what extent, if any, this practice was carried out among Dutch settlers or by those who followed them is not certain, although it seems unlikely that given their tradition of fine brickwork and a love of masonry polychromy, the procedure would have been popular. As architectural historian Hugh Morrison has suggested, the earliest Dutch buildings—those built during the 1600s in

1. The Abraham De Pyster House, 1743

New York City and the Hudson Valley—were often built of yellow, deep red, salmon pink, orange, and even dark purple or glazed black bricks which were characteristically laid in a variety of bonding patterns and often embellished with glazed tiles set into the façades in various patterns.[3] It seems unlikely that walls intentionally laid in such well-planned and colorful fashion would have been painted—at least when new. Later painting could have become the rule, as colorful façades became unfashionable or when worn and tired brick walls required added protection against the threats of weather and wear.

Painting of brick façades seems to have taken firm hold in New York City by the early 1800s. As was generally the case, painting brick seems to have been done as a means of protecting an inferior product or as a way of achieving a more pleasing color when appropriately colored bricks were unavailable. In New York City, and throughout the surrounding area, many aspects of Dutch influence remained well into the nineteenth century, including a love

of order and of fresh paint. An Englishwoman, Sarah Mytton Maury, made the following observations while traveling through the area during the 1840s:

> The most striking and attractive feature presented by American cities, and especially by New York, is their cheerful, bright and daylight aspect . . . . The inhabitants of New York inherit the taste of their Dutch ancestors for fresh paint; every house of any pretension is annually coated with scarlet or grey, the divisions in the brick are picked out with white; the doors and windows are also generally white; and the outside shutters receive a tint of lively green.[4]

The first phase of the Dutch Colonial architectural form is, according to Morrison, the true Dutch Colonial. Largely built of native American brick, these buildings, which originated during the Dutch occupation of the 1600s, but which persisted into the eighteenth century, are most notably characterized by prominent stepped gables whose walls rise above the planes of the steeply pitched roofs.[5] Clues about the painted nature of this phase of the Dutch

The Abraham De Pyster House, Fishkill, New York

house can be derived from a number of sources. Of special interest is a painting of the Van Bergen House, in Leeds, New York, which was painted by John Heaten about 1732. Showing a country version of the Dutch Colonial house form, the painting, used as an overmantel in the Van Bergen House, is said to be the earliest known American genre scene as well as the only one existing of an early American Dutch farmstead. Showing not only the gray stone story-and-a-half house with its gabled ends against a Catskill Mountains backdrop, the painting depicts the house with a characteristic red-tiled roof. Casement windows are framed in bright white painted trim and hung with single-leaf shutters. Shown open, and apparently paneled, they are painted in three colors which include an exterior frame of bright red, an interior panel of black or perhaps very dark blue, and a narrow band of bright white separating them. The split Dutch doors are painted in the same dark color of the shutter panels, with their panel moldings and frames painted white.[6]

The Abraham De Pyster House, which is said to have been built about 1743, is an architectural example of what Morrison terms the last or Flemish Colonial phase of Dutch-inspired domestic building. Displaying an interesting regional characteristic which Morrison claims was common in Dutchess County, the house is constructed of brick at its front and side façades, but of stone at the rear. Apparently this combination was frequently seen from about the mid-1700s and indicates a pref-

erence for brick as a building material.[7] Of special interest and perhaps indicative of the Dutch heritage of well-executed masonry work, are the handsome brick quoins at both of the rear corners and the bold brick surrounds which frame the door and window openings at the rear façade. The effect suggests the importance and impact of the brick façade as well as an interest in a decorative and skillfully manipulated combination of materials to achieve a strong impression.

Color selections for a house such as the De Pyster residence can be derived from a number of sources. Because the house is of decided eighteenth-century origin, the colors selected are not from the bolder, more

primary palette of the 1600s. Wooden trim, as shown on the Van Bergen House, would be appropriate in white, though the shutters, with their handsome panels, might suggest the more colorful hues of the earlier Dutch influence. Window frames and sash could also be appropriately painted in a Spanish brown or a dark blue-gray with the shutters and door frames colored the darker color, relieved by a yellow ochre within the paneled areas. The steps, which are shown of wood construction, would be appropriately painted in the trim color used on the window frames and sash or in a dark-gray color intended to look like slate.

	Scheme A	Scheme B	Scheme C
Paint line	PRATT AND LAMBERT/FORD	STULB/OLD VILLAGE	MARTIN SENOUR/ WILLIAMSBURG
Body	(brick)	(brick)	(brick)
Trim	Museum White 17 GV-W	Colonial White	Robert Carter Tobacco W84-0230
Sash	Museum White 17 GV-W	Colonial White	Robert Carter Tobacco W84-0230
Shutters	frames— Pewter 28 GV-P	frames— Cabinetmaker's Blue	frames— James Moir Shop Fawn W82-1080
	panels— Eagle Tavern Gold 6 GV-M	panels— Antique Yellow	panels— William Byrd III House Ivory W81-1073
Notes	step risers— Pewter 28 GV-P	step risers— Antique Pewter	step risers— Peyton Randolph Gray W82-1086
	step treads— Stone Mill Gray 16 GV-A	step treads— (unfinished wood)	step treads— King's Arm Tavern Gray W83-1076

Consult the Directory of Suppliers, pp. 117-118, for complete manufacturers' names, product lines, and addresses.

2. The Israel Arnold House, c. 1750

DESPITE CONTEMPORARY references indicating that many houses of the 1700s were unpainted, the wide availability of painters' colors and materials suggests that a good number were in fact painted. Well documented by advertisements in Colonial newspapers offering pigments and painters' supplies, house painting of the period is also supported by both written observations and by period paintings. Each of these documents provide a vivid picture of houses painted in a rainbow of tints that seem to have been almost as colorful as those used indoors—a fact that recent research continues to confirm.

Except for the period when the Importation Acts and the subsequent Revolution stopped the flow of pigments, oils, and other painters' supplies, most of the goods necessary were directly imported from England.[1] Though regional color preferences likely prevailed among the colonists, the materials and pigments were apparently available throughout the colonies since English ships often made several stops along the eastern seaboard laden with varieties of goods either ordered by merchants or by private individuals.[2] Colonial newspapers carried frequent advertisements of cargoes of painting supplies, directing them mainly to professional painters who purchased the colored pigments in dry form and then ground and mixed them with oil. The *Newport Mercury,* for example, carried the following advertisement in 1769:

> Just imported from London, in the Snow Tristam, Capt. Shand, and to be sold by Nicholas P. Tillinghast at the Sign of the Mortar in Thames Street. Gold Leaf, Prussian Blue, Vermillion, Verdigrise, Spanish White, Spanish Brown, Spruce, Yellow, Copperas, Logwood, ground Redwood and Red Saunders.[3]

This colorful palette may be compared with a hand-tinted engraving of Newport which was advertised for sale in the *Mercury* twenty-six years later. Illustrated in the engraving are houses in at least five different colors, including red, yellow, gray, blue and, of course, white.[4] Newport colors were apparently unusual enough to have been noted by visitors. One, a French officer assigned to Rochambeau's army near the end of the Revolution, made the following entry in his diary in 1780: "The exteriors of Newport houses are painted divers colors, . . . [which] give a variety pleasing to the eye."[5]

The Israel Arnold House illustrated here represents the quintessential Colonial

	Scheme A	Scheme B	Scheme C
Paint line	—	—	CALIFORNIA/NEWPORT
Body	Benjamin Moore/Historic Colonial Yellow 10	Cook and Dunn/Historic Amber Hall	Gilbert Stuart Brown
Trim	Stulb/Old Village Meeting House White 1101	Stulb/Old Village Meeting House White 1101	Gilbert Stuart Brown
Sash	Stulb/Old Village Fenno House Green 1114	Stulb/Old Village Colonial Green	Gilbert Stuart Brown
Shutters	—	—	—
Door	Stulb/Old Village Fenno House Green 1114	Stulb/Old Village Colonial Green	Gilbert Stuart Brown

Consult the List of Paint Companies, pp. 117-118, for complete manufacturers' names, product lines, and addresses.

The Israel Arnold House, Lincoln, Rhode Island

American house. The earliest portion, seen at the left, was built about 1695 and was eventually finished externally to conform with the appearance of the remainder of the structure constructed during the eight-eenth century.

Of pleasing proportions and of spare yet handsome detailing, the Arnold House is typically Georgian in its symmetry and strict sense of proportion, the latter of which was often carried to precise geometric extremes on more high-style examples. Related both stylistically and regionally to the Vernon (chapter 3) and Bowman-Carney (chapter 4) houses, the Arnold

House is a more vernacular interpretation of the style that places it among the best examples of its type. The long-fronted façade of this rural house indicates a more expansive surrounding than its urban counterparts.

Yellow or straw was a popular house color throughout the 1700s and as such has been used on the Arnold House rendering. Among the most widely used and available yellows of the time was yellow ochre, a pigment composed of clay and hydrated ferric oxide. Though reported to have been relatively dull in appearance, yellow ochre was popular largely because it was readily available and hence inexpensive. The color also had the advantage of being long-lasting, a quality which would have made it especially popular with those who could not afford to repaint their buildings every four or five years.[6]

A contemporary account of the use of yellow ochre is found in an agreement between St. George Tucker and Jeremiah Satterwhite, a painter engaged to work for the prominent Williamsburg citizen in 1798. The agreement stipulates that although the main house was to be painted white, the exterior of the kitchen, a separate building, was to be painted in yellow ochre to which a small amount of white lead was to be added. The same color was to be applied to the dairy.[7]

Color scheme B suggests another popular color used during the mid- to late 1700s and apparently well into the 1800s as well. Rather unusual to twentieth-century eyes, perhaps, the color which we might call "pumpkin" today is decidedly orange and appears to have been used not only on domestic buildings but on outbuildings as well. A "recipe" for its fabrication can be found in a small book published in 1812 by Hezekiah Reynolds, a painter of both houses and ships who claimed over thirty years of experience. His directions indicate mixing red lead with a straw color as the means of achieving orange, the intensity of the color, of course, being controlled by the amounts of the components. Reynolds, who apparently was quite an authority on the subject, suggested adding one pound of lead to every ten pounds of the straw color, the latter made with ten pounds of white lead and one of either spruce yellow or English ochre, "well ground and mixed."[8]

Perhaps the most interesting of all the documents regarding an orange house is a painting by Francis Alexander of Ralph Wheelock's New England farm, painted in 1822. Showing a charming assemblage of dwellings and farm buildings set along the top of a slight ridge, Alexander was meticulous in his color rendering of the structures. Although a large white house with the usual green shutters dominates the scene—as its counterparts did the American landscape—a smaller house quite similar to the Arnold House in form and period is the one which seems to capture one's attention. Painted orange, the building has white trim and a red roof and what seems to be a green door. Interestingly, a barn of the same orange, with white trim and a large red door, balances the composition on the far side of the painting, suggesting that outbuildings were painted as colorfully as dwelling houses.[9]

The roof color shown on Wheelock's orange house may have been an example of a relatively common roof treatment during the 1700s and early 1800s. Once again, the painting agreement between Tucker and Satterwhite provides a clue. Tucker directed Satterwhite to paint not only the roof of the main house, but also a shed and covered way "with Spanish brown, somewhat enlivened, if necessary, with red lead . . . ."[10] This house, still standing in Williamsburg, has been painted in these documented colors.

Suggested as a third and final color scheme for a house of the general period and style of the Arnold dwelling is a Spanish brown for the body as well as for the sash and trim. Widely popular at the time, Spanish brown was used on outbuildings or on "coarse work" where the practical desire to protect the wooden surfaces outweighed both cost and fashion. Recent research by Colonial Williamsburg, for example, has indicated that Spanish brown was not only used on outbuildings or on "coarse work" but at least in one instance on the trim and window sash of a fine brick residence, which despite its stylistic façade and "noble" ownership was, during part of the eighteenth-century, a money-producing rental property.[11] Hence, practicality above fashion.

AMERICAN BUILDING, for the most part, has been an architecture of wood. The popularity of wood for domestic purposes has been a result of its abundance, its ability to be easily worked, its relative economy, and the fact that it lends itself to rapid construction. And, of course, in the hands of skilled craftsmen, wood has always been able to be carved into wonderful forms imitating stone and enjoying wide use because more people were able to work with wood than with masonry. As a consequence, even those who were well able to afford houses of brick or stone often favored buildings of wood.

One of the most interesting features of American architecture is its tradition of style-consciousness in combination with its adaptive nature. Both, of course, speak a great deal about the spirit of the people who built, of those for whom they built, and of the era in which a structure was built. It is not surprising, therefore, that colonial Americans developed a fondness for an exterior architectural treatment which imitated stone, was as fashionable as British work, and, best of all, was adaptable to contemporary conditions. Called rustication, this exterior treatment was simply the covering of a building's façade with wooden boards cut to appear as stone "blocks." To further the deceit, a covering of fine white sand was generally cast across the face of the freshly painted and still wet façade in order to present the feel and texture of cut stone.

The best-known American residence

3. The Vernon House, 1760

with a wooden rusticated façade is George Washington's Mount Vernon. The house was sheathed in this manner by about 1760, several years before it was expanded to the size and appearance that it has today.[1] The wooden façade was not only rusticated but also sanded. Other domestic structures with this type of cladding,—which according to architectural historian William H. Pierson, Jr., may be of uniquely American invention[2]—seem to have been concentrated in the New England colonies. Among the best known are the Jeremiah Lee Mansion in Marblehead, Massachusetts, and the Wentworth-Gardner House in Portsmouth, New Hampshire. A fondness for such artful deceit even appeared in regions quite removed from the larger urban areas, where the embellishment appeared as "trimming" used as quoins or within door enframements.[3] In these cases, the remainder of the house was generally sheathed with wood in the usual fashion so that there was a noticeable contrast between elements of the variously treated wooden façade.

At least one American house, unfortu-

nately destroyed only twenty-two years after its initial construction, reportedly had both stone and wooden rustication as a façade treatment. Malbone Hall, an elegant country house built in 1741 by the wealthy Rhode Island merchant Godfrey Malbone near Miantonomi Hill, was largely constructed of pink sandstone from the builder's own quarry in Connecticut. Two observers who visited the building independently commented in 1744 and 1750 that the corner blocks or quoins of the house were wooden and, like the window frames, painted to imitate marble.[4]

The Vernon House is an an excellent example of a fine eighteenth-century building with a rusticated façade. Built in Newport, Rhode Island, it reached its present appearance at about the same time that Mount Vernon's exterior was covered with this kind of sheathing. Originally said to have been painted brown in imitation of Portland stone,[5] the Vernon House, according to information in the Newport Historical Society, was repainted in about 1782. In a letter from Samuel Vernon to his father, William, mention was made that the

The Vernon House, Newport, Rhode Island

house was being painted the color of pink stone, which the younger Vernon noted was to be achieved with the addition of a small amount of red pigment to white paint. In his reply, William Vernon, apparently concerned about the cost of completing the job, wrote that Barry, who was perhaps a family servant, ". . . could throw on the sand as well as [could] the painter."[6] Actually, sanding a façade *evenly* requires quite a bit more skill than seeding a field of radishes, and one wonders what the final effect was like! In any event, there is the possibility of an interesting historical footnote concerning this repainting procedure. During the previous year, Washington had visited the house when it served as the Revolutionary War headquarters for the French General Rochambeau.[7] Apparently, the house was in need of painting at the time, and one wonders, given the similarity of its facade treatment with that of Mount Vernon, if Washington gave any advice on painting and sanding. Chances are that he did since he was keenly interested in architecture.

The following color schemes represent three alternatives for a house with a rusticated facade or, indeed, for any house of the same style and general period. Admittedly, rusticated facades are uncommon, though houses are more common that have only rusticated corners or details within door enframements. Color scheme A, as illustrated, is similar to that of Mount Vernon. While the Vernon House roof is shown of slate, that of Mount Vernon is of wood and painted the same or approximate color as the doors. Color scheme B evokes the Vernon House scheme of 1782 as discussed above. Color scheme C is intended to suggest the building's original color scheme, which was said to have been an attempt at imitating Portland stone. Peter Harrison's Redwood Library (1748-50), a building in Newport with another rusticated facade, is reported to have been painted in this color as well.[8] In all schemes, the body color has been indicated as the shade for trim, since the intent of this kind of facade treatment was generally to suggest that the entire building was constructed of the same stone. The shutters, of a later style than would have originally been used on the house, are painted green, as they were at Mount Vernon.

	Scheme A	Scheme B	Scheme C
Paint line	CALIFORNIA	FINNAREN AND HALEY/PHIL.	COOK AND DUNN/HISTORIC
Body	Puritan Village White 28800	Mt. Pleasant Pink	Limestone
Trim	Puritan Village White 28800	Mt. Pleasant Pink	Limestone
Sash	Puritan Village White 28800	Mt. Pleasant Pink	Limestone
Shutters	Newport Arnold Green	Pennfield Brown	Mullica
Door	Newport Walnut Room Brown	Pennfield Brown	Bottle Green 281
Other	Wooden roof can be painted to match door.	same as scheme A	Wooden roof can be painted Mullica. An alternate color for door, Mullica or Fort Mifflin Brown.

Consult the Directory of Suppliers, pp. 117-118, for complete manufacturers' names, product lines, and addresses.

4. The Bowman-Carney House, 1761

ALTHOUGH RECENT RESEARCH into colonial America's paint history has yielded a palette of rich and colorful hues, the simple fact is that many domestic exteriors were unpainted. Perhaps this image can best be seen today in the very lovely town of Deerfield, Massachusetts, where several eighteenth-century houses are restored to an unpainted appearance.

Notwithstanding the fact that unpainted wood does not last as long as that which has been painted, many houses were maintained in this condition throughout the 1700s, especially in rural areas. Various contemporary accounts mention this fact or note that those houses which were painted were white. There surely must have been, as well, numbers of houses in stages between the two, with wooden siding showing only the faintest signs of having once been painted. This effect can be observed today at several of the more progressive outdoor museums, where recent curatorial policies have encouraged an accurate portrayal of American life and living environments. At Colonial Williamsburg, for example, one can now see, among the less manicured lawns, building façades which have been allowed to wear and weather in very much the manner of their eighteenth-century counterparts. More than one shop or outbuilding ("outbuilding" here refers to any attendant structure such as a kitchen, laundry, or carriage house) displays a worn exterior finish of whitewash over Spanish brown, the latter color often being used on secondary buildings as a base or priming coat.

The Bowman-Carney House, built in Lincoln County, Maine, in 1761, is a successful rural version of a high-style New England Georgian residence such as the Vernon House shown in chapter 3. Though constructed many miles north of Newport, the Bowman-Carney House displays a careful attention to architectural detail and proportion that characterizes the style and which was a natural part of the housewright's vocabulary during the period.

As indicated in the colored illustration, the Maine house has been given the appearance of the unpainted house of the 1700s. Apparently, the practice of trimming a house in a reddish hue was not uncommon and is said to have a history reaching well back into the 1600s.[1] Recent paint research has revealed that various trim elements, including the cornerboards, fascias, and window frames, were sometimes painted a dull, thin red, a custom that was favored well into the eighteenth century.[2] At Deerfield today one can observe the unpainted façade of the Sheldon-Hawks House (c. 1743) which has a wonderfully warm unpainted façade of weatherboarding highlighted *only* by window sash painted red. As a resident of the region noted about nearby Northampton, Massachusetts: "the only painted houses . . . as late as 1781 were the Dwight House, John Hunt's, Caleb Strong's, Timothy Mathew's, and Ebenezer Hunt's, all with gambrel roofs."[3] Architectural historians William A. Flynt and Joseph Peter Spang have commented that this reference to gambrel roofs suggested the newer, more elegant and "up to date dwellings in town" and, hence, the financial ability of their owners to afford a painted façade.[4]

Color scheme A, as noted, includes both a painted version meant to closely approximate the color of an unpainted façade, and a stained version. In both instances the emphasis is upon our twentieth-century practice of protecting the wood surface of a house. Note, however, that the true function of a stained finish is to allow the substrata to be visible through the coating. Modern stains meant for house façades tend to be opaque. Despite this and the fact that eighteenth-century unpainted façades were apparently untreated, modern stains are a good concession for today's non-museum house and are worthy of consideration in cases where they can be effectively applied.

Color schemes B and C are alternatives based, as well, upon historic examples. Scheme B is similar to the original color selection that has been restored to the Dwight-Barnard House, a gambrel-roofed structure built in Springfield, Massachu-setts, between 1722 and 1733 and later moved to Deerfield. The paint scheme is said to date from the 1750s when the gam-brel roof and elegant swan's neck door surround were added.[5] Scheme C illustrates another authentic combination with a stone-colored body, white trim, and red roof and door, inspired by the original color application on the Silas Deane House (c. 1766) still standing in Wethersfield, Connecticut.[6]

	Scheme A	Scheme B	Scheme C
Paint line	PRATT AND LAMBERT/FORD	MARTIN-SENOUR/ WILLIAMSBURG	FINNAREN AND HALEY/PHIL.
Body	Pottery Brown 12 GV-A	Bracken Tenement Biscuit W81-1064	Independence Hall White
Trim	Secretary House Red 27 GV-A	Bracken House Blue Slate W81-1064	Franklin White
Sash	Secretary House Red 27 GV-A	Nicholson Store Red W86-1081	Franklin White
Shutters	—	—	—
Door	Pottery Brown 12 GV-A	(see note below)	Congress Hall Red
Other	For solid color stains: body— Pittsburgh/Stains Timber Tan SC-70 trim, sash—Sash color includes sash, corner boards, and door. Pittsburgh/Stains Rustic Red SC-61	Trim color includes window surrounds, door surround.	

Consult the Directory of Suppliers, pp. 117-118, for complete manufacturers' names, product lines, and addresses.

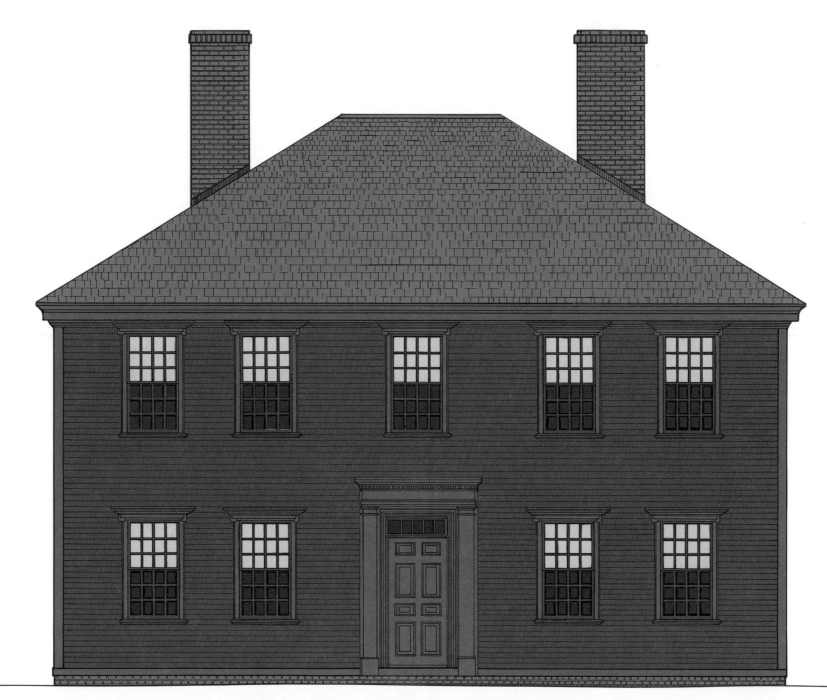

The Bowman-Carney House, Cedar Grove, Maine

The Reynolds House, Providence, Rhode Island

5. The Reynolds House, 1805

ALTHOUGH SOME SCHOLARS question the use of blue on residential exteriors before the 1880s, evidence exists which indicates the color's popularity on domestic façades as early as the mid-1700s.[1] Among the earliest written accounts is a notice which appeared in the *Newport Mercury* on December 19, 1758, advertising the sale or lease of a large house that was painted blue.[2] Several years later, a resident of Deerfield, Massachusetts, one Charissa Ashley, wrote to invite her brother to come and "visit the Blue house some moon shine night."[3] The Ashley House, which still stands in that delightfully preserved town, is, however, no longer painted, and is today an illustration of but another common eighteenth-century exterior treatment—*unpainted* sheathing.

In addition to the written evidence about the use of the color blue, pictorial documentation exists which shows houses with façades painted in that color. For example, a colored engraving of Newport, Rhode Island, made in 1795, includes a blue-gray house among a number of other variously painted buildings.[4] Still later evidence of the continuing popularity of the color blue can be seen in a series of drawings made by Elder Joshua Bussell, a leader of the Shaker community in Alfred, Maine. This collection of precisely painted plans and views, executed between 1845 and 1854, indicates several blue-gray buildings among a number of others painted in red, yellow, and green.[5]

Perhaps the most fascinating of all are the representations of blue-painted houses that appear stitched onto a number of Rhode Island samplers dating from the mid-1700s to the first few years of the nineteenth century. All but one, apparently, are known to have been stitched in Newport, which gives clear indication of the color's popularity in that seaport town. Among the most interesting is a piece worked by Sarah Taylor in 1756 which shows a two-story, two-bay dwelling with brick gable ends and a blue façade. Another, by ten-year-old Anne Anthony made thirty years later, depicts the more usual five-bay house, again in the same color, indicating the popularity of the color's use well after the Revolution.[6]

Charissa Ashley's house was not the only one in Deerfield to have been painted blue. The Wells-Thorne House, originally built in 1751, has been repainted in a sky-blue, which investigation indicates was applied to the façade during the first decade of the nineteenth century. In typical fashion, the

	Scheme A	Scheme B	Scheme C
Paint line	FINNAREN AND HALEY/PHIL.	PRATT AND LAMBERT/FORD	CALIFORNIA/NEWPORT
Body	Belmont Blue	Gallery Stripe Blue 35GV-M	Dudley Grey
Trim	same	same	same
Sash	same	same	same
Shutters	—	—	—
Door	same	same	same
Other	If shutters are used, color would be the same as the body, trim, sash, and doors.	same as scheme A	same as scheme A

Consult the Directory of Suppliers, pp. 117-118, for complete manufacturers' names, product lines, and addresses.

same color was used not only for the body of the house but also for all the trimwork and the door.[7] To twentieth-century eyes, the practice seems severe, though it was a very common painting procedure throughout the period. What it accomplishes, if unintentionally, is to strengthen the architectural detailing as part of the entire aesthetic composition rather than as a separate piece of a larger scheme. It may be that this practice has some basis in the fashions for imitating the monochromatic effect seen on some eighteenth-century stone buildings in which a building material of only one color was used across the entire façade. Another reason for this practice may well have been sheer ease of application. In any case, the effect can be rather handsone if the building to be painted has proportions and detailing as well conceived as that of the Reynolds House, originally built in Providence, Rhode Island, in 1804.

The three color concepts following are all variations of the solid-blue scheme. This monochromatic procedure would be effective with other authentic colors, as well, with care being taken to consider the size, shape, setting, and detailing of the building to be painted. Color scheme A, as illustrated, is the bluest of the range. Scheme B, a sky-blue tint, is similar to the color of the Wells-Thorne House, as discussed above. Scheme C, as a variation, is a color closer to a light gray or blue-gray which in the past was often close enough to have been considered blue.

Harmony Hall, Lawrenceville, New Jersey

HARMONY HALL, BUILT in 1815 in Lawrenceville, New Jersey, is a good, solid example of a domestic stone building of late eighteenth-century inspiration. Constructed in a town not far from Princeton, this house is typical of many which were built in west-central New Jersey, eastern Pennsylvania, and northern Delaware from the last two decades of the eighteenth century into the first two decades of the nineteenth. It is constructed of local stone, which seems most often to have been limestone, with façade colors ranging from grays to browns depending on the origin and type of stone.

Architecturally, Harmony Hall was clearly influenced by Georgian forms while at the same time is infused with elements of the increasingly popular Federal style which developed after the War of Independence. Like the Oliver Culver House, illustrated in chapter 7, this example is possessed of elegant proportions, large window openings with wide panes, and a sparsity of architectural embellishment that, because of its attention to detail, contributes to a façade of both grace and reserve. Buildings like this one, often built by prosperous Quakers and no-nonsense Presbyterians, frequently display a solid, straightforward plainness that is both solidly handsome and richly elegant in their simplicity.

Though many houses throughout this region were built of stone that was meant to be exposed, others, it appears, were covered with a coating of stucco which

6. Harmony Hall, 1815

served both to protect the walls and to provide a decorative finish. In a book entitled *Historical Collections of the State of New Jersey,* published in 1844, what are termed "geographical descriptions" of the state's townships provide interesting clues about the appearance of the area's buildings during the early 1800s. In a description of the state house or capitol at Trenton, for example, mention is made that the building was "built of stone, and stuccoed in imitation of granite."[1] Another description of Tewksbury Township, Hunterdon County, notes that the Evangelical Lutheran Church

	Scheme A	Scheme B	Scheme C
Paint line	STULB/OLD VILLAGE	—	PRATT AND LAMBERT/FORD
Body	(stone)	(stone)	Pewter 28 GV-P
Trim	Meeting House White 1101	Old Village/Stulb Meeting House White 1101	Pewter 28 GV-P
Sash	Meeting House White 1101	Glidden/Historic Cambridge 18104	Museum White 17 GV-W
Shutters	first floor— Meeting House White 1101 second floor—Sugar Box Green 1122	Glidden/Historic Governor's Grove 30874	Museum White 17 GV-W
Door	Meeting House White 1101	Glidden/Historic Governor's Grove 30874	Museum White 17 GV-W
Other	—	—	Stucco over stone is scored and painted in imitation of granite.

Consult the Directory of Suppliers, pp. 117-118, for complete manufacturers' names, product lines, and addresses.

was also "built of stone and plastered."[2] There is no reason to doubt that this practice was carried out on private buildings as well, for indeed many can still be observed with plaster coatings intact. This fashion for imitation carried over to even wood-framed houses in the region. One in particular, built by John Imlay in 1790 in Allentown, New Jersey, had a front façade of finely fitted boards which may have been sanded and painted in imitation of a masonry building. At Harmony Hall, the front façade was recorded by HABS as being stone; the north side (the gabled end at the right) was shown as largely stuccoed. Perhaps this treatment was carried out as a protective measure sometime after initial construction.

Since the primary color of stone houses derives from the hue of the material used in constructing the walls, exterior decoration is dependent upon the colors chosen for trimwork, sash, and window shutters. Following regional custom still practiced on masonry buildings today in the Mid-Atlantic region, the shutters in the illustrated example are shown painted white at the first floor windows and green at the second. This practice seems to date at least to the early nineteenth century. As was common, especially during the 1800s, first-floor shutters were often solid and paneled, providing a practical form of security when closed at night and a decorative quality when open during the day.

Conversely, second-floor shutters, which functioned mainly as a means of controlling light and air, were generally slatted rather than paneled. It is tempting to speculate that these practical uses may, in fact, have dictated the colors of the shutters themselves. For example, when the white paneled shutters were closed at night, the surfaces would reflect light in the already darkened interior that was lit only by an open hearth fire and candles. On the second floor, where the shutters would have functioned during the daytime to shade the interiors, a darker, nonreflective surface would have been the ideal. At night, when these shutters were generally closed, darkness, of course, was the object.

Color scheme B represents an alternative to scheme A and involves painting the sash and changing the color chosen for the shutters. Color scheme C provides a selection for a stuccoed façade "in imitation of granite."

7. The Oliver Culver House, 1817

THE TYPICAL GEORGIAN building form—a two story, five-bay house with central doorway—remained the preeminent architectural model for domestic structures well into the nineteenth century. During the last two decades of the 1700s, however, decoration, both internally and externally, began to take on an altogether different character. Because of the influence of archaeological and architectural investigations in both Greece and Italy, neoclassic detailing came to be appreciated and understood in ways unknown to the Renaissance and Palladian architects whose work had been popular in eighteenth-century America. Fine detailing, well-proportioned elements of elegant richness which were often played against subdued backgrounds, and a general attenuation of architectural features became the hallmarks of this new style. Characterized by an overall feeling of lightness and grace, the style is best known in America as "Federal" because of its development during the early years of the new nation.

Whereas interiors of the period seemed to enjoy a more lavish and vibrant color palette, residential exteriors appear to have been treated with colors that were generally lighter than those of the preceding era. It is possible that lighter colors were felt to be effective in reinforcing the less cumbersome architectural detailing which darker tones might have obscured. Clues for the exterior decoration of residences during this period have been derived from a number of sources, not the least interesting of which is a small book with a long title. *Directions for House and Ship Painting shewing in a plain and concise manner, the Best Method of Preparing, Mixing and laying the VARIOUS COLORS NOW IN USE* was written by Hezekiah Reynolds, a painter of long experience, in 1812.[1] His list of ten exterior colors (he also listed interior shades) was as follows: white, cream, straw, orange, pea-green, parrot-green, grass-green, red, slate, and black. Of the last color, special note was made that it was *not* recommended for painting window sash, the mere mention of which suggests that its use for such a purpose was common. He did note that black was appropriate for painting doors, as were most likely some of the more colorful tints.[2]

The Oliver Culver House, Rochester, New York

Pictorial evidence indicates that one of the most popular colors for exterior work at this time was a light yellow or cream color. Two finely detailed watercolors, now in the collection of the Society for the Preservation of New-England Antiquities, show the Federal-style Elizur Wright House in Medford, Massachusetts. Painted by an unknown artist in 1810, these two views not only provide information about the house's color scheme, but about its landscaping as well. The two-story dwelling is painted a body color of very pale yellow, highlighted with white trim. The prominent chimneys are probably plastered and are painted white, as is the foundation. The central door on both the front and garden façades appears to be pea-green as are the shutters which flank both doors. There are no other exterior shutters.[3] A portrait of a similar house in Castine, Maine, was painted about thirty years later by the well-known artist Fitz-Hugh Lane. His painting of the residence of Dr. Joseph L. Stephens shows a body color of a deeper, though still light, yellow and a front door painted white. Green shutters of about the same pea-green shade hang at each window and at the door. A chimney, which is red, may have also been painted, not an uncommon practice.[4]

Three appropriate Federal-period color schemes are listed, with scheme A shown in the illustration. The yellow door shown in that rendering was inspired by the color recently applied to the front door of Gracie Mansion, the official residence of the Mayor of the City of New York. Originally built by Archibald Gracie during the late eighteenth century, this Federal-style house was meticulously restored, with attempts made to conform to painting practice of the time. In that regard, the porch flooring was left unpainted rather than receiving several coats of paint in the fashion of later practice.[5]

Color schemes B and C provide examples of additional body colors popular at the time.

	Scheme A	Scheme B	Scheme C
Paint line	—	GLIDDEN/HISTORIC	—
Body	Cook and Dunn/Historic Tuscan Ivory	Rushmore 27222	California/Puritan Village Document White 45082
Trim	Pratt and Lambert/Ford Museum White 17 GV-W	St. Michael's 21342	Pratt and Lambert/Ford Museum White 17 GV-W
Sash	Pratt and Lambert/Ford Museum White 17 GV-W	English Tudor 20984	Pratt and Lambert/Ford Museum White 17 GV-W
Shutters	Cook and Dunn/Historic Smithtown Green	black	Cook and Dunn/Historic Commons Green
Door	Cook and Dunn/Historic Colonial Yellow 259	St. Michael's 21342 or black	Pratt and Lambert Museum White 17 GV-W or Cook and Dunn/Historic Commons Green

Consult the Directory of Suppliers, pp. 117-118, for complete manufacturers' names, product lines, and addresses.

The Richard Townley House, Union, New Jersey

WHILE DOMESTIC BUILDING forms in the first two decades of the nineteenth century remained basically the same as they had during the previous century, exterior paint colors appear to have taken a noticeable turn by the century's end. Architectural features became lighter in feeling, more graceful in form, and more delicate in detail with a resulting change in the color palette. Clapboards painted rich creams, warm straws, delicate grays, and pristine whites acted as subtle backdrops for the garlands, festoons, fanlights, and pilasters which proclaimed a refined elegance not previously seen. Even masonry buildings were often painted, sometimes in a bright red with the mortar joints picked out in white as was common in the New York of 1820.[1] Many brick buildings were painted in light grays and buffs as well, and even Boston's State House (1795-98) was painted yellow.[2]

The color scheme for the Townley House is inspired, in part, by one shown in a painting by Francis Guy of Brooklyn, New York. The view, painted sometime near the end of the painter's life in 1820 and entitled "Winter Scene in Brooklyn," is one of several painted by the artist.[3] A similar painting, "Summer View of Brooklyn," includes the same elements.[4] Guy's two wintertime paintings appear to be identical, though they are not. The house which suggested the Townley color scheme is of a yellow-buff color in one painting, while in the second picture it is of a cream shade. Said to have been the dwelling and shop of Thomas W. Birdsall, the gambrel-

8. The Richard Townley House, 1815

roofed house pictured at the far right of the composition is strikingly similar to the Townley House, not too surprising since the form is common to the region in which these two buildings were constructed. In both winter scenes the Birdsall house is shown with dark green slatted shutters on the second floor and white painted paneled shutters at the first-floor windows. The summertime view of the same house indicates green slatted shutters on the first floor, suggesting that the need for summer ventilation may have necessitated replacing the paneled security shutters with ones through which air could flow.[5]

As is often the case, careful examination of paintings like Guy's can reveal a wealth of fascinating details and clues about the

	Scheme A	Scheme B	Scheme C
Paint line	BENJAMIN MOORE	COOK AND DUNN/EXTERIOR	STULB/STURBRIDGE
Body	High Gloss Clapboard Buff	Candlewhite	Towne House Ivory 1123
Trim	Historic Lancaster Whitewash HC-174	Candlewhite	Meeting House White 1101
Sash	Historic Lancaster Whitewash HC-174	Candlewhite	Meeting House White 1101
Shutters	Historic first floor—Lancaster Whitewash HC-174 second floor—Hadley Red HC-65	Gate Gray	Sugarbox Green 1122
Door	Historic Lancaster Whitewash HC-174	Candlewhite	Sugarbox Green 1122

Consult the Directory of Suppliers, pp. 117-118, for complete manufacturers' names, product lines, and addresses.

period they portray. For the architectural historian studying color, it suggests that green was the preeminent shutter color in the early nineteenth century. It also indicates that several buildings, including sheds and stables, were unpainted and that there was a very close relationship between the more elegant life of the street and the every-day-and-necessary life of the adjoining alley. One interesting feature which the Guy paintings reveal is what was apparently a somewhat common practice of painting building façades and leaving sides unpainted. In addition to color information, the architectural clues about rainwater leaders, basement areaways, exterior vestibules, and domestic fencing (which was apparently often unpainted) are invaluable for the restorationist since many of these "everyday" elements have disappeared or been replaced long ago.

The color scheme of the Townley House represents a variation of the usual scheme with dark-green shutters. The choice of a dark-red, nearly brown, shutter color against the buff clapboards suggests shades mentioned by Hezekiah Reynolds in his *Directions for Home and Ship Painting* . . . . Paintings of Boston street scenes, most notably one entitled "The Old State House" painted by James B. Marston in 1801, show numbers of buff-colored brick buildings, including the still extant Old State House (1711-49) itself.[6] Though no buildings are shown with exterior shutters, except one with a bow-windowed shop, several show doors which appear to have been painted a reddish-brown color.

9. Umbria, c. 1829

THIS GRACEFULLY GALLERIED Southern plantation house, located in Hale County, Alabama, is transitional in style from the Federal to the Greek Revival. The date of its construction, 1835, however, places it firmly within the time period during which the ideals of the Greek Revival style reigned supreme throughout America. The colonnade reflects this fascination with Greek forms, but other architectural features of the house are more Federally inspired than Greek.[1] Eliptically fan-lighted doorways, Federal-style dormers, and an overall grace and attenuation of detail characterize the building. As architectural historian William H. Pierson, Jr., has noted of this building type, the orders used for the columns are more often Roman than Greek.[2]

While some have argued that houses of this type were built raised above ground to afford plantation owners a suitable vantage point for viewing their property, the simple fact is that local conditions necessitated the practice. Much of the region in which these houses were constructed is low-lying and consequently damp; the summer climate was hot and humid. The form, said to have been adapted from eighteenth-century houses built in the Mississippi Valley by French settlers was, at least in one respect, uniquely suited to the regional conditions.[3] Broad hipped roofs, overhanging the building on all four sides, provide excellent shelter from the heat and humidity, and, when raised on piers, a dry place upon which to live as well. The concept is romantic—and made more so by the deep, shadowy porches, broad steps leading to the main floor, and the often gracious style of life which centered about such a building. In fact, the very name "Umbria," redolent of antiquity, suggests the idyllic notions that have come to be associated with this building form.

For the most part, the paint color chosen for the exterior decoration of such Southern houses seems to have been white. The charming and precisely detailed paintings of Marie Adrien Persac depict several bayou country houses which support this fact.[4] One well–known house, now owned by the National Trust for Historic Preservation, and built between 1831 and 1834 for the Weeks family, is shown in an 1861

Umbria, Hale County, Alabama

Persac drawing painted white with green blinds.[5] Today Shadows-on-the-Teche is known for its beautifully hued pink brick, white trim and columns, and dark green blinds.

Inspiration for the color scheme of Umbria was derived from an historic house complex recently restored in Saint Martin Parish, Louisiana.[6] Though of smaller size than Umbria, the Henri Penne House is of similar form as well as age. Preserved by a scholar of the area and its architecture, the house and its outbuildings have been re-painted in a variety of colors closely duplicating those originally used. The body color for Umbria's stuccoed façade

is, thus, painted white. Imitating an out-building at the Penne complex, the exterior baseboard and the window sash have been assigned a terra-cotta color, and the wooden lattice between the porch piers has been painted a dark green not unlike the color on the exterior shutters of the Penne house. At Umbria original shutters are not indicated, though they would have been appropriate, if not essential, during the 1800s.[7]

The additional color schemes maintain the use of white for the major walls of the house, but suggest trim and shutter colors that would have been used on houses of similar period and design.[8]

	Scheme A	Scheme B	Scheme C
Paint line	COOK AND DUNN/HISTORIC	COOK AND DUNN/HISTORIC	PRATT AND LAMBERT/FORD
Body	Parchment	Parchment	Whitewash White 9 GV-W
Trim	Bisque	Limestone	Ballroom Tan 21 GV-P
Sash	Cape Russet	Pewter	Eagle Tavern Olive 15 GV-A
Shutters (if used)	Bottle Green 281	Academy Gray	Webster Green 20 GV-A
Door	Bisque	Parchment	Secretary House Green 14 GV-M
Other	baseboard—Cape Russet columns, cornice, step faces, brick—Bisque porch lattice—Bottle Green 281 window frames—Sandstone	baseboard—Pewter columns, cornice, step faces, brick—Parchment	baseboard—Eagle Tavern Olive 15 GV-A columns, cornice, step faces, brick—Ballroom Tan 21 GV-P

Consult the Directory of Suppliers, pp. 117-118, for complete manufacturers' names, product lines, and addresses.

10. The Augustine House, 1834

THE UNMISTAKABLE HALLMARKS of the Greek Revival style—a temple front and a low pitched pedimented roof—are seen on the modest, yet handsome, cottage built in LaPorte, Indiana, in 1834. Scaled both to the pocketbook and to its geographic setting, the Augustine House, like so many others of its size, gives a clear picture of the aspirations of those for whom it was built and of the skill and style-consciousness of those responsible for its construction. While there were far grander houses built in the style throughout the Midwest, and indeed across the country, this house typifies the interest of the general population in an architecture that had universal meaning within the American experience—in this case the democratic ideals of the Greek city states and the development of American democracy. The style was adapted to banks, churches, courthouses, and even tiny law offices. The example shown was probably inspired from a design in an architectural handbook, copies of which went west with a professional class of settlers. The centrally pavilioned Augustine House, balanced by flanking wings, is interesting to compare with the frontispiece for "A Modern Country Villa" shown in Minard Lafever's 1833 edition of *The Modern Builders' Guide.*[1]

For the most part, houses built in the Greek Revival style were painted white in order to emphasize the effect of a marble-faced temple, or so the general belief has been. Contemporary accounts and paintings showing houses of the period bear this out, although there were some variations. The color scheme illustrated has been inspired from one discovered several years ago as original to Bulloch Hall, a Greek Revival house in Roswell, Georgia, built in 1840. In writing of the house in 1974, architectural historian William Seale noted that the colors used were an illustration of the interest that was growing at the time in the more colorfully painted façades of the original Greek temples.[2] While the body color remained white at Bulloch Hall, the trimwork, including that around the doors and windows and the window sash, were painted the color of straw. This same color was also used on moldings along the cornice and at the pediment. Spanish brown, a color that had been popular during the eighteenth century, was used on the horizontal fascia along the porch at the base of the columns. The shutters were painted a dark, nearly black, green to complete the scheme. As the illustration indicates, the Bulloch Hall scheme has been closely followed except for the color of the shutters, which are shown in a brighter green consistent with that seen in many paintings.[3] Originally, the four front columns of the Bulloch House were marbleized in shades of blue over white. While likely very effective on that house, this treatment has been eliminated from our small house because of its less than high-style design and because its columns are square.[4]

Color scheme B provides an example of a more classic color treatment consisting of a white body and white trim. Scheme C proposes a color treatment that might have been selected in imitation of a building stone, most likely chosen for use on a house that has been plastered or stuccoed to appear as masonry block. In all three color schemes, the doors have been painted and grained, a treatment that all nineteenth-century painters were able to provide. The shutters on schemes B and C have been painted dark green, as at Bulloch Hall.

	Scheme A	Scheme B	Scheme C
Paint line	CALIFORNIA	GLIDDEN/HISTORIC	COOK AND DUNN/HISTORIC
Body	Puritan Village Birchwood 45044	St. Michael's 21342	Limestone
Trim	Newport Colony House Gold	St. Michael's 21342	Parchment
Sash	Newport Colony House Gold	St. Michael's 21342	Bottle Green 281
Shutters	Puritan Village Forest Green 47125	Sleepy Hollow 42774	Bottle Green 281
Door	grained	Bedford Road 15554 or grained	Bottle Green 281 or grained

Consult the Directory of Suppliers, pp. 117-118, for complete manufacturers' names, product lines, and addresses.

The Augustine House, LaPorte County, Indiana

The Francis M. Dimond House, Bristol, Rhode Island

11.   The Francis M. Dimond House, 1838

IN OCTOBER OF 1849, a few days after her arrival in New York, Frederika Bremer, the Swedish diarist, sailed up the Hudson River with none other than Andrew Jackson Downing (1815-52).[1] As they floated up-river in a gold and white steamer towards Downing's "beautiful villa of sepia-colored sandstone . . . ,"[2] Bremer was just beginning to write the observations which in 1853 were published here as *The Homes of the New World: Impressions of America.* Though the book falls short of describing the specifics of building types the contemporary architectural historian might wish, Bremer's many observations are tantalizing hints—and indeed impressions—of American life and its setting during the ante-bellum period.[3]

Among Bremer's first observations about the nature of the American home is the following which seems to capture some of the air of idyllic romanticism that was typical of the era:

> The river was full of life. Wooden roofed steamboats, . . . passed up and down the river, . . . while hundreds of larger and smaller craft were seen skimming along past the precipitous shores like white doves with red, fluttering neck ribbons. On the shores shone forth the white country houses and small farms. I observed a great variety in the style of building, many of the houses were in the Gothic style, others like Grecian temples . . . . Many private houses, . . . were of a soft gray and of a soft sepia tint.[4]

One imagines, of course, that Downing was pointing these things out to Bremer, and we can only guess that he must have taken much satisfaction in noting the many houses painted in grays and sepias, colors which he so strongly advocated. Downing, however, was not as fond of the Grecian "temples" which caught Bremer's eye.[5] Part of the Greek Revival's popularity, beyond its associations with classical Greece and, therefore, democratic America, rests on the fact that the architectural package, as it were, was relatively easy to construct. In its simplest form, the Greek Revival house is a typical American wood-framed box which might be turned gable-end forward to effect a "temple-like" form—whether or not columns were added. Other details such as wide, flat cornices, moderately pitched roofs, two-paneled doors, and large six-over-six windows were simply the basic ingredients or embellishments which any carpenter could easily adapt. Elaborate moldings and two-storied columns with capitals were further refinements which, though requiring more skill to construct than the basic stylistic elements, were still easier to concoct than the emerging Gothic-styled counterparts.

Originally built in 1838 in Bristol County, Rhode Island, the Francis Dimond House is a textbook example of the full-blown Greek Revival house and is similar to many Bremer saw along the Hudson's shores. It was designed by Russell Warren

	Scheme A	Scheme B	Scheme C
Paint line	—	—	PRATT AND LAMBERT/FORD
Body	Cook and Dunn/Historic Gothic Rose	Cook and Dunn/Historic Limestone	Museum White 17 GV-W
Trim	Cook and Dunn/Historic Parchment	Cook and Dunn/Historic Limestone	Museum White 17 GV-W
Sash	Cook and Dunn/Historic Gothic Rose	Cook and Dunn/Historic Essex	Secretary House Red 27 GV-A
Shutters	California/Newport Nichols Rose	Pratt and Lambert/Ford Webster Green 20 GV-A	black
Door	California/Newport Nichols Rose	Pratt and Lambert/Ford Webster Green 20 GV-A	grained or black
	or grained	or grained	
Other		Portico columns, architrave, and pediment moldings— Cook and Dun/Historic Parchment	

Consult the Directory of Suppliers, pp. 117-118, for complete manufacturers' names, product lines, and addresses.

(1783-1860), a prominent architect who once had a brief partnership with Alexander Jackson Davis (1803-1892), a master of both the American Gothic and Greek Revival styles. Warren, acting upon the wishes of his patron, sheathed the front façade with granite. The front steps were also constructed of granite (noted as "pink granite" in the HABS survey drawing). The irregular stone foundation was faced with concrete and probably scored and colored to appear as masonry block, and perhaps as the pink granite.

All other surfaces of the Dimond House, according to notations taken during the building's survey, were painted white. Though likely a visual survey at best, the use of white on the wooden siding at the sides and on the trim and sash would be consistent with period practice. White—because of its association with marble—was the color of choice for the Greek-styled house. The window shutters, however, would likely have been painted either one of the various greens, a dark green–black, or black, all of which are evidenced in contemporary paintings. The front door, shown as originally designed, would likely have been finished to imitate a dark, richly grained wood or to match the shutters.

One of the most interesting features of the Dimond House is the small Gothic-style addition added on the left during the 1840s. Despite its small size, the addition presents a somewhat contradictory element to the house that suggests a certain confusion in the mind of the building's owner as to which style was more fashionable and hence acceptable at the time the addition was built. Of special architectural importance, it is the kind of subsequent addition which preservationists claim most worthy of preservation because it defines the use and development of a building over time. In our example, its presence has also served as the clue to the paint scheme selected.

Although most Greek Revival houses were probably painted white, there was some latitude then in practice. A building of similar design, renovated in the mid-nineteenth century by Davis, Warren's former partner, is one of those exceptions in color. In 1852 Davis received a letter from a former client, the wealthy New York merchant Robert Donaldson. Donaldson wrote that instead of building the Gothic villa that Davis had proposed for him, he wished instead to "[give] up all purpose of Building a Villa upon the Heights [and] . . . to live [and] die in this *Greek Temple*!"[6] The house referred to as a temple was most likely designed by architect Robert Mills about 1820 and is still standing. Known as Edgewater, it has six two-storied Doric columns across its front. Donaldson's letter requesting Davis's assistance in "improving" the house and its grounds stated his intentions of adding a picture room and library as well as an "elegant greenhouse" to the building. By 1854 Davis had designed the library—an octagonal addition attached to the building's left side. Of Gothic form in shape and Italianate style in detail, the one-story addition gives the house an unexpected asymmetricality and makes it appear less static. The greenhouse, to have balanced the composition on the right side, was never constructed.[7]

The façade of the central Greek Revival structure is sheathed in a warm pinkish-colored stone, most likely sandstone, which is probably original to the building. After the library was added, the addition was stuccoed and is today painted a warm pink sandstone color which matches the stone façade of the main building and is a treatment and color of which Davis would have surely approved. It seems plausible, therefore, that farsighted homeowners, like Donaldson, would have made attempts to "improve" their habitations not only with additions in more fashionable styles, but would have painted them with fashionable colors as well.

Color scheme A for the Dimond House suggests that, in addition to the sandstone-colored walls, a darker sandstone color be used for window shutters.[8] A similar color has been used at Edgewater. Color scheme B follows Bremer's observations concerning the presence of houses painted in "soft gray" and suggests the color of a stone which could be used on a similar façade. Scheme C recommends a more classic combination of a white body with black shutters and dark-red sash, the latter color being one, like black, popular for sash during the first several decades of the 1800s. A similar scheme with dark-red sash can be seen today on the Concord, Massachusetts, house once occupied by Emerson.

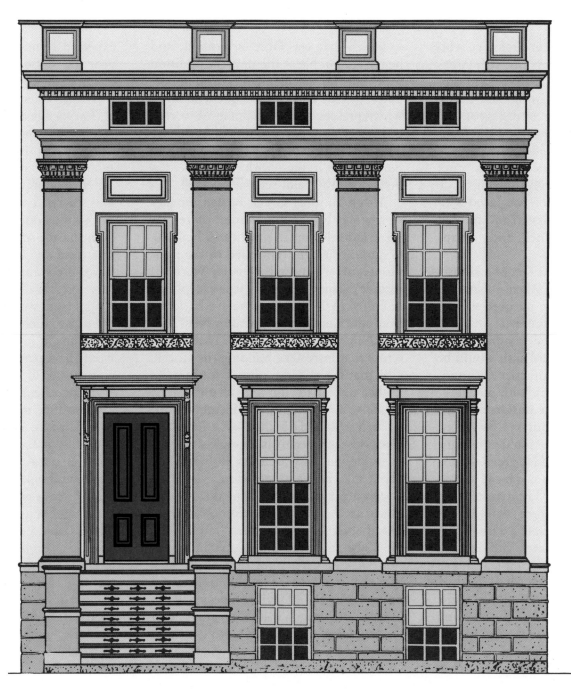

The David Alling House, Newark, New Jersey

12. The David Alling House, 1841

BY THE TIME THAT David Alling's house was constructed in 1841, the Greek Revival style had taken firm root on the American architectural scene. Nonetheless, many buildings continued to exhibit a reliance upon the styles of the recent past. In some instances, this conservative preference was a result of an owner's taste, of regional custom, or of local builders' preference for familiar styles and construction procedures.

The Alling House, unfortunately no longer extant, is a good example of the transitional link between the Federal-style house and the full Greek Revival building. While the house is largely evocative of the latter idiom, the refined detailing around the first-floor windows and door reflects the more ornate decorative quality of the neoclassical elements that preceded the Greek. The chaste, spare, and severely handsome features which exemplify the

	Scheme A	Scheme B	Scheme C
Paint line	CALIFORNIA/PURITAN VILLAGE	CALIFORNIA/PURITAN VILLAGE	—
Body	Birchwood 45044	Colony White 47144	California/Puritan Village White 28800
Trim (pilasters, cornices)	Manchester Gray 45061	Colony White 47144	California/Puritan Village White 28800
Sash	Dove Gray 45051	Black 47102	California/Puritan Village Rockwell Red 28832
Shutters	—	—	—
Door	Forest Green 47125	Black 47102	Benjamin Moore/MoorGard and MoorGlo Essex Green 43

Consult the Directory of Suppliers, pp. 117-118, for complete manufacturers' names, product lines, and addresses.

later style are easily seen in the building's general solidity, in its strongly emphasized pilasters, in the decorative features below the second-floor windows, and in the wooden rail above the cornice.[1]

In neighboring Manhattan, only a few miles from Newark, New Jersey, where Alling built his house, rows of brick Greek Revival townhouses were the fashionable norm during the 1830s and '40s. Often built in blocks or runs of five or more, these identical buildings relied upon one another for their architectural impact.[2] Though many were originally intended to be unpainted, changing ownership through the years diluted the original impact of uniformity not only through architectural additions but in some instances by the application of coats of paint which may have been used as preservative coatings for the bricks themselves. Sadly, the reliance on sandblasting in the recent past as a means of removing paint and restoring the brick façades has often caused not only the removal of paint but the fired-on protective coating of the face brick as well. The result has been a wall with little protection against the ravages of moisture.

Unlike most of its New York City neighbors, the Alling House was constructed of wood above a masonry base finished with a coat of stucco and scored. A black-and-white photograph of the building taken in 1936 indicates that the house was painted some medium tone, with the trim and window sash painted in a darker shade of perhaps the same color. Possibly a reasonable facsimile of an earlier scheme, which was likely colored in imitation of stone, the color selection and placement appears to have been rather straightforward except for a few elements which may have been a product of late–nineteenth-century inspiration.

Color scheme A suggests a color imitative of a fashionable, but costly, stone such as a granite or limestone. The pilasters and other decorative elements have been highlighted in a similar shade. Since many houses in this style featured free-standing columns and were painted to imitate marble, scheme C suggests such a *faux* treatment. In both schemes B and C, the sash has been painted in colors darker than the body, a not uncommon period practice.[3]

13. The Vanderpool Farmhouse, 1848

THIS STORY-AND-A-HALF HOUSE is not unlike the thousands of simple frame dwellings constructed throughout the United States between c. 1830 and 1870. These buildings were characterized by a simple yet handsome dignity related to the Georgian style of the preceding century but firmly respondent to the Greek Revival style which began to exert itself during the 1820s. Not always featuring columned, pedimented fronts, the stylistic elements include bold, wide cornices, handsome door enframements, and large well-proportioned windows placed to affect the overall scheme. Two-paneled doors, like that shown at the right wing of the Vanderpool Farmhouse, are typical of the period.[1]

In the nineteenth century, as today, architectural styles and theories about domestic arrangements were disseminated throughout the country in relatively inexpensive and readily available periodicals and books. One of many influential books was *Rural Architecture*, published in 1852 by the firm of C. M. Saxon. Throughout the book's nearly four hundred pages, its author, Lewis F. Allen, provides a great deal of information concerning the physical arrangement of the American farmstead, including ideas for the design and color of farmhouses as well as information about the most suitable dogs and geese for the barnyard. Like others of his era, Allen saw the subject of rural architecture as encompassing many aspects, all tied together in an interesting philosophical manner that is truly nineteenth-century.[2]

Unlike others who discouraged the use of white for painting houses, Allen began his color essay by noting that white paint was not only time honored, but was also effective as a wood preservative since it reflected the damaging rays of the sun from wooden clapboards.[3] Darker colors, among which were some of those he termed "sooty-daubs," had the opposite effect, he noted, and gave the rural farmstead a rather unbecoming "tomb-like" appearance.[4] This is not to say that Allen was completely against the use of more subtle shades on domestic buildings. He wrote that if the colors were both cheerful and softly toned and *not* applied with any thought to imitate stone or brick, the "warmth and comfort" they would impart would be acceptable.[5] Of his distate for im-

The Vanderpool Farmhouse, Prospect, Wisconsin

itation, Allen commented: "all imitation or device which may lead to a belief that it may be other than what it really is, is nothing less than fraud, not criminal we admit, but none-the-less a fraud upon good taste and architectural truth."[6] In regards to the way architects spoke a half century later, Allen's words, like those of A. J. Downing, sound prophetic.[7]

The color scheme for the building illustrated is based on that used for the recently restored Abraham Lincoln House in Springfield, Illinois.[8] The body color is a light golden brown. Dark–green shutters, though *not* of the darkest green advocated by Downing, complement the softness of the brown and the color of the door, the latter painted and grained to imitate mahogany. The Lincoln House scheme shows that the trim and sashwork were painted several shades darker than the body, a practice widely followed during the 1800s. In typical fashion, the chimneys have been painted the body color since, very commonly, brick was not considered the proper color or grade to be left unpainted. In another common practice, the foundation has also been painted—in this case, a dark gray which has also been used as the color of the front steps, both risers and treads.[9] Where foundation work is natural stone, as it is in the Vanderpool Farmhouse, the masonry is best left unpainted. Paint schemes B and C are alternative choices of other warmer colors which Allen would have likely approved.

	Scheme A	Scheme B	Scheme C
Paint line	—	Cook and Dunn/Exterior	Cook and Dunn/Historic
Body	Pratt and Lambert/Ford Susquehanna Sand 10 6V-M	Quaker Brown	Cottage Beige
Trim	Pratt and Lambert/Ford Susquehanna	Taupewood	Cobblestone
Sash	Pratt and Lambert/Ford Susquenanna	Jersey Buff	Essex
Shutters	Martin Senour/Williamsburg Banjamin Powell House Green	Bottle Green 281	Essex
Door	grained	grained	grained

Consult the Directory of Suppliers, pp. 117-118, for complete manufacturers' names, product lines, and addresses.

14. The David B. Cartwright House, 1852

AT FIRST GLANCE the Darius B. Cartwright House might be mistaken for a New England farmhouse of the early 1800s. In fact it was built in Oregon in 1852, and is one of a number of domestic structures still standing along the West Coast that nostalgically reflect the Eastern roots of their inspiration.

If the Cartwright House was constructed by a builder using local materials, he was surely a carpenter of both considerable skill and stylistic knowledge. The house, built near Eugene, is dignified by a denticulated cornice, corner pilasters, and shouldered architrave moldings around its windows. All exhibit a reliance on the architectural symbols of the neoclassical styles which had all but passed from the Eastern scene by this time. The handsome door surround, however, exemplifies the more current, and yet even then waning, Greek Revival style.[1] This, in conjunction with the curiously delicate porch, contributes to a building representative of the conservative nature of American architecture. In addition to the building's form and its implied center-hall plan, the house, like so many others of its period, is a pastiche of the classic American domestic structure.

The color scheme for this house is suggested, in part, by its charming naiveté. As was not uncommon during the nineteenth century on rather simple buildings, the white-painted body is outlined with a color, in this instance green, which also highlights the architectural features of which the owner would have been justifiably proud. This practice is supported in numbers of contemporary photographs, indicating that only one trim color was used. In this example, further inspired by a view of a similarly painted house on an 1852 tavern sign,[2] the handsome paneled doorway is highlighted with a touch of red, suggesting a modest amount of show without extravagance.

Next to white, green was probably the most popular exterior color in nineteenth-century America.[3] Of especial interest is the color's ubiquitous use on shutters and the effect it produced inside a house when the shutters were closed.[4] Used to regulate shade and to assist in keeping out drafts, closed shutters across open windows on a hot summer's day effectively cut down on the heat and glare that could make a non-air conditioned home so uncomfortable. Contemporary accounts most often term the internal effect of the closed shutter "cooling,"[5] a condition which would be difficult to achieve when sunlight beat against a white shutter. At the same time, green shutters would present a clean appearance when their outside faces became inside window treatments. White or light-colored shutters are simply hard to keep clean, especially if they are slatted.

A. J. Downing, in *Cottage Residences* (1842), advised that shutters be painted the "darkest green," while many Americans apparently preferred those of a bright or "mineral green."[6] A documented restoration that shows an example of this latter shade is the Ebenezer Hinsdale Williams House in Deerfield, Massachusetts, which copies a color applied about 1820.[7] Mineral green, according to an 1825 issue of a Boston periodical, *The New England Farmer*, has "a very strong body . . . . "[8]

Two alternate schemes are as authentic as color scheme A and would have probably found more favor with Downing. Scheme B presents a body of very light gray; and scheme C, of the lightest drab or fawn. In both instances, trim is indicated as several shades darker than the body. Shutters, if present, would be painted a black-green. If a white body with a colored outline other than green is desired, giving the same effect as scheme A, a sepia or gray-brown would be a good period selection.

	Scheme A	Scheme B	Scheme C
Paint line	Cook and Dunn/Historic	California/Puritan Village	Benjamin Moore/High Gloss
Body	Parchment	Manchester Gray 45061	Clapboard Buff 55
Trim	Bottle Green 281	Dove Gray 45051	Jamesboro Gold HC-88
Sash	Bottle Green 281	Dove Gray 45051	Thornewood White HC-27
Shutters	—	Forest Green 47125	Chrome Green 41
Door	Parchment, Bottle Green 281, Colonial Red 280	Dove Gray 45051 or grained	Thornewood White HC-27 or grained

Consult the Directory of Suppliers, pp. 117-118, for complete manufacturers' names, product lines, and addresses.

The David B. Cartwright House, near Lorane, Oregon

The Elwood Evans House, Olympia, Washington

15. The Elwood Evans House, c. 1862

THE ELWOOD EVANS HOUSE, built sometime between 1860 and 1865 in Olympia, Washington, is a solid, though slightly unusual, example of a mid-nineteenth-century form. With its simple gable end fronting the street, the house seems to allude to the form of the classically porticoed Greek Revival house, though it is both simple and more easily constructible. Given the rugged frontier setting of Olympia at the time, a full-blown Grecian temple, even if feasible for early settlers, would have seemed frivolously out of place.

First settled around 1849, Olympia became the capital of Washington territory in 1853. Seven years later the town, by then incorporated, had a population of nearly 1,500 and was the territory's largest settlement.[1] Since Olympia was founded in large numbers by New Englanders via the Midwest, it is hardly surprising that the architecture which first developed there was reminiscent of the simple Greek Revival buildings known to the settlers back East. Easily reproduced, these simple structures were a practical match for the skills of the carpenter-pioneers who had vast reserves of native timber at their disposal. Both lumbering and shipping became the area's major businesses and the basis of many a fortune as well.

The most prominent early building constructed in Olympia was, quite expectedly, the territorial Capitol. Built in 1856, it has aptly been called a building of "the frontier Georgian style."[2] Of simple form and wood-framed construction, the townhall-like building was decidedly Greek Revival in character, with chaste, severe detailing, wide, flat cornices, and a low-pitched roof. An early, though undated, photograph shows the two-story building painted white with dark, possibly black, painted window sash and what appears to be a natural wood or wood-grained door.[3]

Not unlike the Capitol, the Elwood Evans House, built only four years later, represents what must have been a prominent residence for a family of some importance. Similar in appearance to the territorial governor's "mansion," built about the same time, the Evans house was likely constructed by the same hand.[4]

Numbers of old photographs taken in the Western frontier region testify that many structures were either unpainted or painted white. A photograph of nearby

	Scheme A	Scheme B	Scheme C
Paint line	—	GLIDDEN/HISTORIC	BENJAMIN MOORE/ MOORGARD AND MOORGLO
Body	Pratt and Lambert/Ford Carriage Green 8 GV-A	Tarrytown 16503	Sandpiper 59
Trim	Cook and Dunn/Historic Mullica	Bedford Road 15554	Antique Bronze
Sash	Cook and Dunn/Historic Mullica	English Tudor 20984	Black 80
Shutters	Cook and Dunn/Historic Commons Green	Sleepy Hollow 42774	Essex Green 43
Door	Cook and Dunn/Historic Mullica or grained	Bedford Road 15554 or grained	Antique Bronze or grained

Consult the Directory of Suppliers, pp. 117-118, for complete manufacturers' names, product lines, and addresses.

Seattle, taken about 1861, shows an amazingly neat and orderly assemblage of smallish wood-framed buildings. Most of them are white and surrounded by picket fences.[5] It is, therefore, quite logical to surmise that houses of a certain size, and hence of larger cost, were likely to have been painted from the start. Early black-and-white photographs show an odd building here and there painted in another color, though what it was, of course, is impossible to guess.

While white would have been the most commonly seen house color, buildings like the Elwood Evans House, especially if erected in more settled regions, could certainly have been painted in the varieties of colors that A. J. Downing and his followers then advocated. The three selections provided are suitable to the period and have been inspired by their recommendations. As suggested by many contemporary photographs, color schemes B and C provide for the painting of the window sash in darker colors than the surrounding trim. Of course, a body of white would always be authentic, and an interesting contrast would be to paint the sash black or dark red and the shutters a very dark black-green.

Octagonal House, Afton, Minnesota

In a book entitled *A Home for All or The Gravel Wall and Octagon Mode of Building,* Orson Squire Fowler (1809-1887) extolled the virtues of the eight-sided house. Originally published in 1848, the book was popular enough to enjoy at least six printings by 1856.[1] Within its pages, Americans were introduced not only to the merits of this architectural form but also to a particular style of living that could only have been palatable within the context of the reformed ideals of the period. Popular in Europe as well, Fowler's book is even reported to have had a following in the Far East. Across America its influence is said to have resulted in the construction of well over a thousand octagonal dwellings, many of which are still standing.[2] These ranged in size from the very large, of which Fowler's own three-story house in Fishkill, New York, may have been the largest, to small one-story cottages with sides barely ten feet long.[3]

One wonders if the idea of an octagonal house could have developed as easily in a setting other than mid-nineteenth-century America. The period, one in which Americans were becoming more assured of a national identity, was, in part, a product of the romantic idealism which developed in reaction to the logic and reasoned position of the preceding century. As historian John A. Garraty has suggested, the spirit of the new age was characterized in large measure by a population that was intuitive, emotional, patriotic, individualistic, and ingenuous—a people who felt the need to

16. Octagonal House, c. 1868

effect change.[4] It was, among other things, an age of reform and reformers, a time when religious communes were popular, educational methods for the instruction of the deaf and blind developed, the period when the temperance movement took great strides, and an era of abolitionism and prison reform. Strong ideas about vegetarianism, personal exercise, and hygienic housing captured the American mind. It was also a period in which some of the country's greatest writers flourished. Among them, Ralph Waldo Emerson, though not against the notion of reform itself, wrote of some of the zealots as "narrow, self-pleasing, conceited [people] who affect us as the insane do."[5]

It was to this America that Fowler introduced his ideas of good, decent, and affordable housing for all. A phrenologist by profession, he made a great deal of money by writing and lecturing about this

	Scheme A	Scheme B	Scheme C
Paint line	GLIDDEN/HISTORIC	CALIFORNIA/PURITAN VILLAGE	FINNAREN AND HALEY/VICTORIAN
Body	Western Reserve 65333	Victorian Rose 45054	Jamestown Red
Trim	Weathervane 65333	White Horse Tavern 47152	*Lime White
Sash	Weathervane 65333	Chestnut Brown 47127	Lime White
Shutters	if used— Tankard 41762 or Weathervane 65333	if used— White Horse Tavern 47152	—
Door	Tankard 41762	White Horse Tavern 47152	Brown
Other			*As per battens shown on several period examples.

Consult the Directory of Suppliers, pp. 117-118, for complete manufacturers' names, product lines, and addresses.

pseudo-science. His belief in "inhabitive-ness" as the major phrenological trait led him to the conviction that everyone should have a home, and an economical one.[6]

Fowler was especially interested in concrete construction, both because he believed that it was economical and because he reasoned that it was a solution to a dwindling supply of wood. The octagon, he noted, contained "one-fifth more room for its wall,"[7] and, he argued, was more akin to natural shelters which he claimed were generally spherical. In addition, he advocated the introduction of hot and cold running water, speaking tubes, filtered water for drinking, and flush toilets as necessary amenities. Ironically, his own eight-sided house, a concrete structure erected in 1848, was razed not even a half-century after it was completed because of sewage leaking through the walls.[8]

Not surprisingly, Fowler had a theory of color which he presented with an emphasis upon practicality. He began his brief treatment of the subject with "the recipe for a superior whitewash" that had been applied to the White House.[9] While he did not discourage the use of white as an exterior color, Fowler did note that whitewash could be easily shaded by the introduction of a number of materials which would result in pink, a reddish stone color, and a slate color which he especially favored for exterior work. In addition, he also referred to yellow ochre as a durable color choice, pointing out as an example a yellow house in Philadelphia that had weathered well for a decade.[10]

The Thomas House in Afton, Minnesota (circa 1868), is shown painted a slate-blue color. As Fowler noted in his book, the choice of the final shade should be in part determined by the personal taste of the owner.[11] The trim, shown painted a darker shade of gray, has been selected following A. J. Downing's dictum that darker shades be used for trim work.[12] The doors, which would be very appropriate if painted and grained, are, as an alternative, shown painted a lighter gray than the trim. The fact that Thomas, surely familiar with Fowler's book, built his octagon of wood probably did not bother the phrenologist much at all. He believed that an octagonal house built of wood was far better than none at all.[13]

Color schemes B and C are also authentic period schemes. Scheme B stipulates a body of yellow ochre, recalling Fowler's mention of the color.[14] Scheme C is a lighter color still, one that would have been called a light drab and which would provide a good ground for the play of light and shadow on the board and batten sheathing. In both schemes, dark-green shutters would be appropriate.[15]

17. 723 Congress Street, c. 1844–56

THE THREE-BAY, two-story house illustrated has, to all appearances, the look of a city residence. Its raised basement, which may be a later addition, the arrangement of the façade, and the street-facing gable suggest a house built to fit a narrow city lot.

Simplicity is the key word to describe 723 Congress Street, Chicago. And yet, though the house was built for a modest sum, it is not without a number of architectural features which give it a certain sense of dignity generally lacking in its modern counterparts. The tall parlor-floor windows, the Egyptian Revival battered door surround, and the wide fascia at the roof cornice exhibit an awareness of proportion and detail which were a part of the vocabulary of the nineteenth-century builder-craftsman.

Without a doubt, 723 Congress Street (circa 1844-56), like the thousands of other houses constructed in mid-nineteenth-century Chicago, was built through the process known as the "balloon-frame technique." One of America's most significant contributions to the art of building, this technique refers to a system of simple light-frame construction rather than the heavier braced-frame technique which was the norm before 1830. The availability, as well, of factory-made nails and machine-sawn wooden members revolutionized the building trades, simplified the construction of houses, and answered the needs for quickly-built housing in boom-growth areas.[1] Of course, the very term "balloon" refers to the rapidity in which buildings constructed in this manner were able to rise.

As originally recorded by HABS, the house illustrated was drawn without exterior shutters. These have been included here, however, to indicate a color selection as well as to give the house a more decorative appearance. At the ground floor level, which likely contained the dining room at the front and the kitchen behind it, exterior shutters were generally a necessity, both for security and privacy.

The use of red in the color scheme shown in the left–hand illustration may be surprising. However, it is known that red was a common color, at least in rural districts, during the first half of the nineteenth

723 Congress Street, Chicago, Illinois

century. One such indication can be seen in a winter scene painted by George Henry Durrie in 1858 and entitled "Winter Scene in New Haven, Connecticut."[2] In it, Durrie depicts a simple farmhouse painted an almost terra-cotta red. An additional hint concerning the use of this color comes from Lewis F. Allen's *Rural Architecture,* published in 1852. At the end of his essay on "Outside Color," Allen writes:

> There is one kind of color prevailing to a great extent in many parts of our country . . . which . . . is a monstrous perversion of good taste. That is the glaring red, made up of Venetian red, ochre, or Spanish Brown, with doors and windows touched off with white . . . [It is] a perver-

sion of everything harmonious in the design. We eschew *red*, therefore, from everything in rural architecture.[3]

Of course, Allen was concerned about the use of red in rural settings since he felt that it did not harmonize with nature. Perhaps he would forgive us—or even approve—our using the color in the city!

Color scheme B, shown to the right, presents a combination more consistent with mid-nineteenth-century color preference. A house with a drab-colored body, trim of a darker hue, and perhaps shutters of dark green would have been in agreement with the palette of theorists like Allen and A. J. Downing. Scheme C, which is not illustrated, provides a selection in grays.

	Scheme A	Scheme B	Scheme C
Paint line	BENJAMIN MOORE/HIGH GLOSS	PRATT AND LAMBERT/FORD	PRATT AND LAMBERT/FORD
Body	Garrison Red HC-66	Sarah Jordan Brown 11 GV-M	Pewter 28 GV-P
Trim	Cliffside Gray 74	Whitewash White 9 GV-W	Stone Mill Gray 16 GV-A
Sash	Cliffside Gray 74	Whitewash White 9 GV-W	Veranda Gray 34 GV-P
Shutters	Park Green 40	—	—
Door	panels— Cliffside Gray 74 frame—Garrison Red HC-66	Whitewash White 9 GV-W	Stone Mill Gray 16 GV-A
Other	door surround, window lingels, and fascia— Cliffside Gray 74	door surround, window lintels, and fascia— Wainscot Olive 24 GV-M	

Consult the Directory of Suppliers, pp. 117-118, for complete manufacturers' names, product lines, and addresses.

18. Greystone, 1859

AMERICAN INTEREST in the Gothic style developed during the 1830s and, at least to some extent, survived throughout the nineteenth century. Like other popular styles of the period, the Gothic complemented the tenor of the times, evocative as it was of a romantic idealism that was architecturally adaptable to wooden construction. Its association with the religious aspects of the larger culture cannot be understated nor can its associations with the chivalrous ideals which were made popular, in part, through Romantic literature.[1] Conversely, other revival styles, such as the Egyptian, were less popular and pervasive though their development was approximately concurrent with the Gothic Revival. Some historians have suggested that associations made with the Egyptian Revival style were partly to blame. A critic in the *North American Review* in 1836 wrote that this style was "an architecture of embalmed cats and deified crocodiles." and not identifiable with the American experience.[2]

A large part of the responsibility for the widespread dissemination of interest in the Gothic Revival is due to the publications of Andrew Jackson Downing. *Cottage Residences* (1842), as well as subsequent books, secured his fame as well as the growth in popularity of the Gothic-style house. Happily for Downing, as well as for the history of American building, his alliance with the well-known architect Alexander Jackson Davis (1803-1892) encouraged the construction of many buildings which had the imprint of this master designer. Best known for the stone masterpiece "Lyndhurst," which still stands beautifully restored above the Hudson at Tarrytown, New York, Davis was able to provide Downing with the designs of modestly scaled houses which appealed to the ways of life and pocketbooks of many rural Americans. Downing's books, in some editions reprinted well into the 1870s, enjoyed wide circulation and, as a result, directly influenced the design of houses all across the country.[3]

Among Downing's most interesting published comments are those made concerning exterior colors. While houses constructed of stone were certainly those which he considered most ideal, he realized that building with this material was not always feasible or affordable. As a result, his comments are instructive for the paint-

	Scheme A	Scheme B	Scheme C
Paint line	COOK AND DUNN/EXTERIOR	MURALO/RESTORATION	BENJAMIN MOORE/ HIGH GLOSS
Body	(natural stone)	(natural stone)	(natural stone)
Trim	Gate Gray	Pewter Cup 13C-2T	Essex Green 43
Sash	Gate Gray	Pewter Cup 13C-2T	Essex Green 43
Shutters	—	—	—
Door	Gate Gray or grained	Pewter Cup 13C-2T or grained	Essex Green 43 or grained
Other	Awning colors— Lexington Gray and Colonial Red 280	Awning colors— Winter Sky 39A-2P and Hollyhock 51C-4D	Awning colors— Hawthorne Yellow HC-4 and Georgian Brick HC-50

Consult the Directory of Suppliers, pp. 117-118, for complete manufacturers' names, product lines, and addresses.

Greystone, Pevely, Missouri

ing of wooden houses as well as those covered with stucco which, most generally, was scored to appear as masonry block. Regarding such a stone house as Greystone, built in Peveley, Missouri, in 1859, Downing would have advocated painting the wooden trim to appear as if it were stone, and most likely several shades darker than the stone used for the main walls. A photograph of Greystone, taken in 1940, shows that the trim was painted in this manner at that time, possibly indicating that the original scheme had been maintained over the years. Color scheme A follows Downing's plan.

Two alternate suggestions for painting the trimwork on a Gothic house of stone are also given. Color scheme B suggests a lighter gray more consistent with the lighter stone used in combination with darker stone for the construction of the walls. Color scheme C calls for a trim of a sepia-colored hue consistent with Downing's taste and with the general character of the style itself. In all cases, naturally stained or painted and grained doors would be appropriate. The metal awning hood over the front door is painted in an authentic manner.[4] Colors used for such features may vary according to personal taste, but should complement the colors of the walls and trim and be consistent with period choices.

THE HISTORY OF ARCHITECTURE in the American West is one of the most fascinating chapters in this country's building history. Part of this fascination rests partly with the "romantic" nature of the pioneer experience itself, with the tales spun around the log cabin, and with the high adventure that has always been a major current throughout the history of western settlement.

During the very earliest years, architecture, or more preciesely building, was a haphazard affair. Shelter from the elements was the primary concern, and to that end anything and everything that could be used for such purposes was employed. The sod house, which became a common building form in parts of the Midwest, comes most quickly to mind. Along the West Coast, and especially in the settlements established by mid-century fortune seekers, shelter took many forms, at least according to one contemporary account of Jacksonville, California, in 1850. The observer wrote about materials as diverse as logs, canvas, woolen blankets stretched between poles, and even burrows cut into hillsides which were sometimes protected by combinations of logs, canvas, and roughly constructed fences.[1] Despite the implied squalor, the picture is nonetheless engaging and was apparently quite a common scene.

Architectural historian Harold Kirker has noted that some of the early California settlers, a large number of whom were miners, actually managed to house themselves in small wood-frame buildings.[2] Ap-

19. The General Vallejo House, c. 1851

parently, some of these structures were even covered with roughly cut shingles or boarding as further protection against the weather, though few, if any, were probably painted. In more than a few cases, wood and materials for some of the first built structures were salvaged from wooden ships that were slowly rotting in San Francisco harbor. In other instances, more seaworthy vessels were floated to shore, beached, and then outfitted as hotels, boarding houses, and whatever else was needed.[3] When the housing situation became even more desperate, those who could afford to do so imported houses from the East Coast, Great Britain, Australia, and even China. Some of these were of iron, and various reports note that several were adorned with fashionable Gothic details, and often painted white with brown trim. One well-to-do New Yorker is said to have had a house, complete with furniture, shipped from Baltimore at a cost of about $90,000.[4]

The charming Victorian Gothic woodframe house that is illustrated was erected in Sonoma, California, about 1851 but ac-

tually built in Boston several years before. One of three identical houses that were possibly in the same shipment, Lachryma Montis or Tear of the Mountain, as this house was called, is said to have cost the princely sum of $60,000.[5] Owned by the prominent General Guadeloupe Vallejo, the house surely stood in sharp contrast with the majority of houses that sheltered others. It represents one of a small yet significant number of buildings that were surprisingly fashionable, given the developing nature of the region.

Most of the painted houses erected in the area at the time were probably white with green shutters. Contemporary accounts bear this out as does the fact that in newly settled areas more "fashionable tints" and a wide variety of pigments were likely to have been unobtainable, at least at first.[6] On the other hand, there were both architects and settlers within the region who were aware of the current fashions in more settled areas. These people expressed a decided interest in architecture from the earliest days of settlement.[7] Goods were eventually obtainable, and, if entire build-

The General Vallejo House, Sonoma, California

ings could be shipped to California, paints, pigments, and other painting materials could have been ordered despite their cost.

The color selection for the General Vallejo House represents an ideal choice for the style and period of building since houses of this type were common in most areas of the country. Color scheme A is a buff or straw color, with dark brown for the trim and dark green used for the shut-ters. Scheme B follows a combination similar to that of Mosswood, pictured in chapter 20, except that in place of the trim of dark rose, dark green has been suggested, not unlike the original scheme on the Bowen House in Woodstock, Connecticut (1846).[8] In each case, the doors can either be painted, as specified, or grained to imitate oak.

	Scheme A	Scheme B	Scheme C
Paint line	BENJAMIN MOORE	MURALO	STULB/BREINIG
Body	High Gloss Clapboard Buff	Restoration Indian Tan 12C-24	Dawn Gray 10-478
Trim	High Gloss Falcon Brown 1238	Georgetown Dark Green 363	Lead Color 10-494
Sash	MoorGard/MoorGlo Tobacco Brown 61	Restoration Burgundy Dash 70A-1A	Cherry Red 10-567
Shutters	High Gloss Chrome Green 41	Georgetown Dark Green 363	Dark Green 12-735
Door	MoorGard/MoorGlo Tobacco Brown 61 or grained	grained	grained

Consult the Directory of Suppliers, pp. 117-118, for complete manufacturers' names, product lines, and addresses.

20. Mosswood, 1864

THE J. MORA MOSS HOUSE is, without a doubt, one of the finest examples of the Gothic Revival style in California, if not on the West Coast. Constructed in 1864 for pioneer Moss, the house was designed by Stephen Williams, himself a pioneer and an architect with an eastern education and no small talent. Williams is perhaps best known for the design of Parrott's Granite Block in San Francisco, completed in 1852.[1] His design for Mosswood, as the house was originally known, indicates both the popularity of the style in newly settled regions as well as the sophistication of the design and building industry soon after initial settlement. The small section at the right front was reportedly added some years after construction and, though of different scale, maintains the general architectural character of the house.

The Moss House is constructed of wood, though the style suggests a building of stone. The façade, made of smooth redwood planks, was originally finished with a covering of fine white sand which had been strewn across the surface soon after the last coat of paint was applied. Specifi-

cations for the house's construction, including directions for painting, indicate that the finished structure was to receive "three coats of fine Atlantic white lead and linseed oil . . ." before the application of the sand which was intended, of course, to give the surface a stone-like texture.[2] Whether or not a colored pigment was mixed into the white lead is uncertain, though it seems likely that some color was added. Enough had been written at the time by A. J. Downing and others of the unsuitability of white that an architect of Williams's stature would have probably chosen buff or tan as suitable "stone-like" colors.

The suggested color scheme illustrated was inspired by a variety of sources and offers an authentic alternative to those colors which Downing mentioned in *Cottage Residences* (1842). Downing was very specific in his recommendations, and *Cottage Residences* includes a plate of six colors considered appropriate for cottage and villa exteriors. Labeled A through F, the first three colors are shades of gray, from lightest to darkest, and the last three of drab or fawn.[3] But not everyone was likely willing to follow the suggestions of a so-called "authority." Most surely followed their own preferences and tastes as to suitable colors with which to paint their houses.

Other writers of architectural books, like Lewis Allen, mentioned the use of color as well. In *Rural Architecture* (1852), published most likely as a response to the popularity of Downing's books, Allen advised: "A wooden country house, together with its outbuildings, should always be of a cheerful and softly toned color—a color giving a feeling of warmth and comfort; [with] nothing glaring or flashy about it."[4] While Allen did not get as specific as Downing about shades, he did mention the suitability of drab which could be highlighed with trim shades of a darker or lighter tone, and of the appropriateness of a warm russet for painting brick, a color he likened to undressed leather.[5]

The inspiration for our color scheme is, in part, derived from the wonderful Gothic Revival house of the Bowen family, built in Woodstock, Connecticut, in 1846. Though similar in size to Mosswood, and similarly detailed, the Bowen house is sheathed instead with board and batten siding, a common exterior treatment that was said to achieve a sense of verticality most suitable to the style. The house has a recently repainted body color of light rose and trim of a very dark green, both colors very close approximations of those originally chosen for the façade.[6] The scheme illustrated, which borrows the body color, follows the

suggestion of Lewis who would probably approve of the trim being painted a darker shade than the body.[7]

The additional schemes are also appropriate period alternatives. Scheme B calls for a buff-colored body reminiscent of a Downing drab, while scheme C, suggests the fondness for grays which imitated stone.

	Scheme A	Scheme B	Scheme C
Paint line	COOK & DUNN	GLIDDEN/HISTORIC	—
Body	Historic Gothic Rose	Tarrytown 16503	Cook and Dunn²Historic Somerset Gray
Trim	Exterior Quaker Brown	Bedford Road 15554	Cook and Dunn/Historic Pewter
Sash	Exterior Quaker Brown	Bedford Road 15554	Glidden/Historic Cambridge 18104
Shutters	—	—	—
Door	Exterior Tudor Brown	Bedford Road 15554 or grained	grained

Consult the Directory of Suppliers, pp. 117-118, for complete manufacturers' names, product lines, and addresses.

Mosswood, Oakland, California

The James D. Roberts House, Carson City, Nevada

21. The James D. Roberts House, 1859

AMERICAN ARCHITECTURE is often most engaging when its forms are "adapted" from more "high-style" prototypes. These reinterpretations or local variations of buildings from either published materials or someone's recollections often fascinate the observer because of the manner in which they take the essential elements of a style and treat them as individual pieces on a façade. Such is the case with the James D. Roberts House, pictured here.

Built in Carson City, Nevada, in 1859, the Roberts House maintained the symmetrical rhythm of the typical American dwelling while becoming a "sample board" for many of the major elements of the Gothic Revival style. Termed "Carpenter Gothic" by some because of a relative ease of construction and decoration, the house displays a pleasing collection of label lintels, lancet windows, fanciful barge-boards, and Gothic-paneled doors. Of particular interest are the small, turned gable finials which are especially meek in comparison with those of Greystone (chapter 18) and Mosswood (chapter 20). Their lack of vigor suggests the timid and conservative hand of a craftsman who, though aware of stylish trends, was cautious in the actual process of design and fabrication.

Color selection for houses of this style and type is of relatively wide scope. White, despite what A. J. Downing and his contemporaries wrote, would surely be acceptable because white was commonly used for every sort of dwelling. Trim of white or green would be appropriate in this case. More colorful choices would include a scheme like the one illustrated or others from the Downing palette of light grays, drabs, or fawns.[1] Any of the color selections shown for the buildings in chapters 16 through chapter 21 would be authentic as well.

	Scheme A	Scheme B	Scheme C
Paint line	BENJAMIN MOORE/HIGH GLOSS	GLIDDEN/HISTORIC	COOK AND DUNN/EXTERIOR
Body	Clapboard Buff	Oregon Trail 15783	Lexington Gray
Trim	Jamesboro Gold HC-88	Bedford Road 15554	Gate Gray
Sash	Greenfield Pumpkin HC-40	Tarrytown 16503	Bottle Green 281
Shutters	if used— Chrome Green 41	if used— Sleepy Hollow 42774	if used — Bottle Green 281
Door	Park Green 40 or grained	Bedford Road 15554 or grained	Bottle Green 281 or grained

Consult the Directory of Suppliers, pp. 117-118, for complete manufacturers' names, product lines, and addresses.

22. The J. Stratton Ware House, c. 1865

IF ONE ELEMENT RUNS as a thread throughout the history of American domestic architecture, it is surely the persistence of the Georgian-inspired symmetrical plan and façade. A clear example of this can be seen in the J. Stratton Ware House, which, though Georgian in inspiration, is characterized by architectural features popular from around the middle of the nineteenth century. Of a general Italianate style, with elements of the Second Empire added for good measure, a house of this type is often mislabeled a "center-hall Colonial," largely because of its form. In reality, a combination of elements such as the window sash, which at the first floor are actually french doors, and the steeply pitched, Gothic-inspired central peak at the roof indicate the characteristic eclecticism that became the hallmark of the period. Located in Cape May, New Jersey, the house was built in 1868.

Exterior colors for a house of this period and form may be chosen from a wider palette than one might imagine. Though certain theorists of the time would have disapproved, painting the body white, with white trim and green blinds, would be quite authentic. Greens, which varied according to taste, ranged from those of a bright mineral variety to those with a dark, almost blackish, tint and would have been used, as well, on the latticework fronting the porch.

The color selection shown here, though authentic to the period, probably did not appear as frequently as the white and green combination. The use of yellow as a body color and green blinds has been documented in several period paintings and seems to have appeared as a color combination during the early 1800s.[1] The painting which inspired this example is a richly detailed portrait by Emil Foerster of what is believed to be the Robert B. Sterling family, that was probably exhibited at the Pittsburgh Art Association soon after its completion in 1859.[2] Depicting a family in front of a house quite similar to the Ware House (except for the fact that it had only three windows instead of five across the front), the portrait—most recently reproduced in *The Magazine Antiques* (June, 1988)—is most interesting in that it illustrates the close color relation between the house and its natural surroundings—a

The J. Stratton Ware House, Cape May, New Jersey

wild, and yet controlled, landscape dominated by moss greens, browns, russets, and ochres.[3]

In addition to the scheme mentioned above, alternate color selections could follow those suggested for the Vanderpool Farmhouse (chapter 13), the Elwood Evans House (chapter 15), or the General Vallejo House (chapter 19).

The porch roof has been redrawn to show a treatment quite popular during the period—painting in stripes to evoke a tented structure. Examples of this practice can be seen in several period photographs and architectural drawings, as well as on restored porch roofs.[4] Contrasting colors were painted either directly onto the roof itself or, as A. J. Downing noted in *Cottage Residences* (1842), directly onto canvas attached to either light iron or wooden frames affixed to the façade over certain windows.[5] Conceivably, painted canvas could have formed the covering of many porch roofs and, especially in summer, would have presented a shady and welcome retreat from the heat and glare of the sun.[6]

	Scheme A	Scheme B	Scheme C
Paint line	BENJAMIN MOORE/ HIGH GLOSS	—	COOK AND DUNN/HISTORIC
Body	Colonial Yellow 10	Pratt and Lambert/Ford Bayberry 23 GV-M	Parchment
Trim	Thornewood White HC-27	Pratt and Lambert/Ford Bayberry 23 GV-M	Limestone
Sash	Thornewood White HC-27	Pratt and Lambert/Ford Museum White 17 GV-W	Essex
Shutters	Park Green 40	Benjamin Moore Essex Green 43	Black
Door	grained	grained	grained
Other	porch roof striping: Pratt and Lambert/Ford Lynchburg Green 48 Platinum Gray 71	porch roof striping: Ballroom Tan 21 GV-P Secretary House Green 14 GV-M	porch roof striping: Cranberry Moss

Consult the Directory of Suppliers, pp. 117-118, for complete manufacturers' names, product lines, and addresses.

23. The John H. Shoenberger House, 1848

AT THE TIME OF ITS CONSTRUCTION in 1848, the John H. Shoenberger House must have been among the most elegant in Pittsburgh. While it is tempting to pigeonhole the house as stylistically Italianate, a closer look reveals its inspiration from a number of nineteenth-century sources. Its gentle and elegant bow fronts, not especially evident in the illustration, are reminiscent of Federal-style work. Concurrently, evidence of the Greek Revival, which had waned by the time the house was completed, is seen in the pediment above the cornice with its paneled central block. Italianate features, which dominate the entire composition and unify the whole, are best seen in the restrained classicism of the façade upon which the classically formed stone window hoods and door surround are deftly positioned. The house is typical of its kind in its eclecticism and inherent conservatism, both of which work curiously well together and say much about the social atmosphere of Pittsburgh a decade before the Civil War.

One of the characteristic features of many Italianate-inspired houses is the use of a stucco cement as a façade treatment. In the illustration of the Shoenberger House, scored lines have been restored to the original HABS drawing to indicate the typical manner in which the building façade would have been finished. (Without scoring, the house would have a far different character.) On much original work still extant, lines etched into the surface in imitation of joints in stone coursing were practical as well as fashionable. Practically, incised lines provide a type of control system which checks large cracks or unevenness in plaster application. Aesthetically, scoring also has the effect of preventing the wall surface from appearing too bland over wide areas.[1]

In the eighteenth century, stucco was often applied to masonry façades as a protective coating. Even brick houses of the very wealthy—thrift often dictated a soft brick—were sometimes covered with a hard cement plaster, probably scored in many instances to appear as fashionable Portland stone.[2] In his well-known diary chronicling experiences as a tutor on a Virginia plantation, Philip Fithian wrote in the 1770s about the stuccoed façade of the elegant Nomini Hall, the center of a vast estate. Noting dimensions and architectural character, Fithian commented that the house was covered with "a strong lime mortar" and that it was "perfectly white."[3]

Many of the clues which we have about the exterior finish and color of Italianate-style houses of the 1800s come from both extant examples of the type and the writings of A. J. Downing. Downing noted the excellence of brick as a building material, but decried its "offensive hue."[4] As a solution, he almost always recommended painting the brick some "agreeable tint" or covering a wall of rough brick with cement stucco. In *The Architecture of Country Houses* (1850) he recommended that the stucco be made of a composition of lime and sand and that it be applied only to buildings with overhanging eaves since water might seep behind the stucco surface of a wall not thus protected.[5] Apparently, the builder of the Shoenberger House was unconcerned about water seepage since the house has no overhanging eaves.

The color of the stucco was generally determined by the application of pigment to the mixture before its application to the wall. In this manner, the color was integral with the material itself, though in several extant examples which have been examined, the coloring agent has leeched out or faded over the years. Consequently, regular painting applications have often been made to these façades with the result that the scoring which has naturally weathered over the years is often completely obliterated.

Downing, not surprisingly, recommended coloring stucco to imitate stone colors—and always light shades. In one instance he suggests the addition of a small amount of yellow ochre to the rough-cast mixture to produce an agreeable " fawn-colored shade . . . more agreeable to the eye than white."[6] The scheme illustrated is reminiscent of this suggestion. The doors, consistent with period practice, are shown grained, and the sash and window frames are colored to match the implied wood color of the door. The cast-iron grilles in the attic windows, as was customary, are painted green.[7]

Color scheme B follows Downing's suggestions for painting a brick façade several shades lighter than the color of its natural stone trim.[8] Scheme C suggests a color imitating a stone similar to the pink-hued sandstone of certain regions. Sash and windows are similarly colored.

	Scheme A	Scheme B	Scheme C
Paint Line	COOK AND DUNN/ HISTORIC	COOK AND DUNN/HISTORIC	COOK AND DUNN/HISTORIC
Body	Cottage Beige	Lamplight Cream	Cobblestone
Trim	Essex	Sandstone	Cobblestone
Sash	Chestnut	Sandstone	Classic Ivory
Shutters	—	—	—
Door	Chestnut or grained	grained	grained
Other	cast iron at cornice— Commons Green		

Consult the Directory of Suppliers, pp. 117-118, for complete manufacturers' names, product lines, and addresses.

The John H. Shoenberger House, Pittsburgh, Pennsylvania

MUCH OF THE DOMESTIC ARCHITECTURE of the third quarter of the nineteenth century defies a clear and definite categorization into any one specific style. The house shown in the illustration demonstrates this dilemma, belonging as it does to both the Second Empire and the Italianate styles and owing much of its overall form to the survival of the time-honored American attraction for the symmetrically designed center-hall house.

In general terms, the Second Empire style, popular during the 1860s and '70s, is best characterized by Mansard roofs, towers and belvederes, classical detailing, pediments over doors and windows, and quoins at exterior corners which strengthen the illusion of stone construction. The Italianate style, most popular during the 1850s and whose elements were often compatible with the Second Empire, is best identified by low-pitched roofs, wide overhanging eaves supported by elaborate cornices with brackets, quoins or pilasters at exterior corners, and segmentally arched door and window openings.[1]

The John Muir House, still standing in Martinez, California, and said to have been constructed in 1860, exemplifies a hybrid form commonly seen throughout the country. The painting scheme for this type of house has been inspired by a number of regional sources. Writing about the unsuitability of white as an appropriate house color, A. J. Downing noted that no credible landscape painter would ever place a white house in the midst of a painting.[2] However, a large painting by George A. Frost, now

24. The John Muir House, c. 1860

owned by the California Historical Society, contradicts this statement. The vast white Italianate house of William Chapman Ralston in Belmont, California, built in 1864 and possibly designed by pioneer architect Henry Cleveland, was depicted by Frost in 1875. The painting shows the house to be even whiter than it probably was because of its setting amid the verdant green of the well-tended lime and ilex groves which reportedly cost the owner over a million dollars to develop. Barns and other outbuildings are also painted white.[3] The house is still extant.

A second regional example of the white-painted house is the residence of one-time San Francisco bartender James C. Flood, whose Nevada silver-mining ventures enabled him to build Linden Towers, in Menlo Park, California, in 1878. Reports are that the house, now unfortunately gone, was known as "Flood's Wedding Cake," not so much for the architectural embellishments which dripped from its complex façade, but because it was painted white.[4]

The Muir House, as a representative example of a Second Empire-Italianate

	Scheme A	Scheme B	Scheme C
Paint Line	FINNAREN AND HALEY/ VICTORIAN	CALIFORNIA/PURITAN VILLAGE	PITTSBURGH/HISTORIC
Body	Monterey	Colony White 47144	Mission Gray 2756
Trim	Monterey	Colony White 47144	Mission Gray 2756
Sash	Black	Black 47102	Pine Mountain 7336
Shutters	if used— Medium Green	if used— Forest Green 47125	if used— Springfield Rifle 7755
Door	(natural finish) or grained	(natural finish) or grained	(natural finish) or grained

Consult the Directory of Suppliers, pp. 117-118, for complete manufacturers' names, product lines, and addresses.

hybrid, is shown painted a "glaring white." Consistent with documentary evidence, all trim and architectural decoration has also been painted white. The window sash, which in this example is shown painted black, would also be authentic if painted a very dark green or even a bronze green, as suggested by Daniel T. Atwood in *Atwood's Country and Suburban Houses*, published in 1871.[5] Doors, commonly painted and grained throughout the century, could properly be stained if the quality of the wood so merited. The exposed foundation, which in true nineteenth-century fashion would not have been covered by foundation shrubbery except possibly at the corners, has been shown painted gray to approximate the color of the roof. Where a slate roof of more than one color is found, paint the foundation—if so required—the major color in the roof, not the color of the accent slates. Wooden roofs, which may also have fancifully cut pieces, could be painted in at least two colors, or simply in a shade of gray, red, or even dark green.

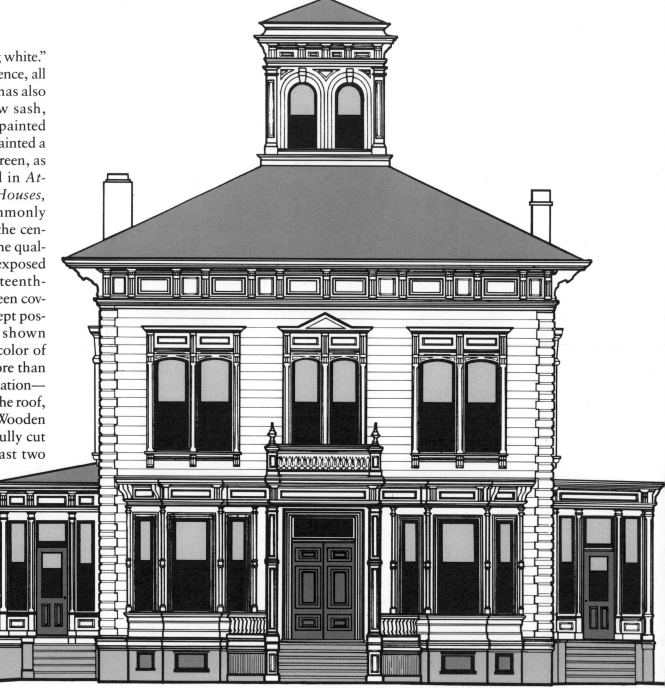

The John Muir House, Martinez, California

The Lew M. Meder House, Carson City, Nevada

25. The Lew M. Meder House, c. 1875

IT IS NOT UNCOMMON to find throughout the scattered towns of the West numbers of modestly sized and even small houses which mimic the more exuberant architectural detailing generally seen on larger dwellings in the East. The reasons behind this seem to indicate at least two things about a frontier society. First, there was an interest in establishing a style-consciousness akin to that of the more established areas of the East and Midwest. Secondly, there was a strong influence from architectural handbooks which commonly stressed the idea that good, decent, and even stylish housing was possible for people of every circumstance. At the same time, architects and master builders were among the pioneers who settled the West and, from the start, exercised a pervasive influence in the architectural climate of newly founded towns.[1]

The Lew W. Meder House, constructed during the late 1870s in Carson City, Nevada, exemplifies the best of the Italianate–Second Empire styles. The rusticated boards at the corners forming quoins and the well-detailed cornice indicate the craftsmanship of a master adept in not only constructing such intricate work but in combining the features in such a well-proportioned way. The architectural elements, however, seem borrowed from a larger, more costly residence.

An appropriate color scheme for a building of this style could, of course, include any of those listed for the John Muir House (chapter 24), since both houses are of the same style. While there may be a temptation to highlight certain architectural features more exuberantly than the scheme indicates, it is often advisable to treat small houses of this kind with care, lest the strength of the architectural detailing break down into a number of individual pieces.

In addition, any of the A. J. Downing colors, including drabs and fawns, would work effectively since their popularity persisted well beyond mid-century.[2]

	Scheme A	Scheme B	Scheme C
Paint Line	—	BENJAMIN MOORE	CALIFORNIA/PURITAN VILLAGE
Body decorative panels	Pittsburgh/Historic Mission Gray 2756	High Gloss Clapboard Buff	Antique White 28820
Trim ©1	Pittsburgh/Historic Old Silver 3757	MoorGard and MoorGlo Sandpiper 59	Putnam Ivory 28835
Trim ©2	Pittsburgh/Historic Hammered Iron 4760	MoorGard and MoorGlo Black 80	Rockwell Red 28832
Shutters and Sash	Finnaren and Haley/Victorian Medium Green	MoorGard and MoorGlo Chrome Green 41	Forest Green 47125
Door	Pittsburgh/Historic Hammered Iron 4760 and panels in Mission Gray or all grained	MoorGard and Moor Glo Sandpiper 59 or grained	Forest Green 47125 or grained
Other	roof— Finnaren and Haley/Victorian Medium Green	roof— MoorGard and MoorGlo Chrome Green 41	

Consult the Directory of Suppliers, pp. 117-118, for complete manufacturers' names, product lines, and addresses.

UNLIKE MOST OF THE HOUSES illustrated in this book, the John N. A. Griswold House is one of the great masterpieces of American domestic architecture. Designed by Richard Morris Hunt (1827-1895), an architect best known for the Vanderbilt family mansions Biltmore (1890) and The Breakers (1892-95), this simple and yet complex wooden building is especially noteworthy for its expression of an inner structure on an outer façade. Though merely suggesting structure, the implication of this organic quality is achieved in a manner that is at once straightforward yet decorative.[1]

Like the Breakers, the Griswold House was built in Newport, Rhode Island, as the summer residence of a prominent family. Constructed between 1861 and 1863, the house, still standing, is representative of the stylish architecture that has long characterized this elegant seaside town. The preeminent example of what has come to be called the Stick Style for its implied "stick-built" construction, the building reflects both A. J. Downing's interest in an architecture of "truthfulness"[2] and the nineteenth-century taste for a fashionable style.

Hunt has the rare distinction of having been the first American architect to be trained at the École des Beaux Arts in Paris. While there, he became very familiar with the major architectural styles to which he later referred in designing his best-known stone palaces and his numerous public commissions. During the same period

26. The John N. A. Griswold House, 1861-63

Hunt was also exposed to the revival of interest in the vernacular half-timbered house which was then sweeping through France and Germany. Hunt is said to have received the Griswold commission while on his honeymoon trip to France.[3]

Though the design for the Griswold House may seem "medievally inspired" to some, it derives from other sources as well. The building's picturesque lines and exposed wood framing are very much in the mid-nineteenth-century American tradition.[4] Hunt was surely familiar with Downing's interest in external structural expression, in his use of board and batten siding as a more correct "expression of strength and truthfulness," and in the use of exposed members in various published designs for "Swiss" cottages.[5]

The exterior color scheme of this Stick-style house has been derived from a number of sources. An early photograph of the Griswold House indicates that the body was painted in a much lighter shade than the exposed framing.[6] Other contemporary photographs of similar houses show the same effect, with some having even darker contrasts, the intention apparently being to emphasize the implied structure. A photograph of Newport's Thomas F. Cushing House (c. 1869) illustrates an interesting variation. Its architect, George C. Mason, was likely responsible for suggesting a color scheme in which both the body below the second floor line and all of the house's decorative timbering were painted the same dark tone in extreme contrast to the lighter color of the body above the second floor line. Exterior shutters were apparently painted in the same dark tone which, on the first floor, created a monochromatic, and very somber effect.[7] Conversely, on both the Griswold House and nearby Coles House, which Hunt designed in 1869, the exterior shutters were painted in what appear to have been the two tones of the house—the frames being of the darker color and the moveable slats of the lighter body color.[8] The houses designed by Hunt are superb architectural compositions and their color arrangement, consistent across the entire façade on both floors, contributed to a lyric lightness and an overall coherence which reinforced the use of the exposed framing system.

The color scheme illustrated was in-

The John N. A. Griswold House, Newport, Rhode Island

spired both by the color contrasts implied in the photographic records and by Hunt's known fondness for architectural polychromy.[9] While most lasting evidence of this interest can be seen in some of his masonry buildings, the colorful slate roof on the Griswold House (slightly simplified in the illustration) indicates a domestic application as well. A proposed elevation for Olana, which Hunt was to have designed for the painter Frederic Edwin Church in 1867 (it was later designed by Calvert Vaux), illustrates this polychromatic scheme on a masonry house.[10] However, most evidence of this colorful and patterned exterior decoration is best found on some of Hunt's larger built masonry commissions. A photograph of the Presbyterian Hospital administration building in New York City, designed between 1869 and 1872, shows a rich decorative exterior composed of red brick and white stone, a combination which one architectural historian has admitted is difficult to appreciate today.[11] Nonetheless, the exterior illustrates the period's love of color and pattern, a richness easily translatable to wood. That translation is illustrated on the Presbyterian Hospital by an enclosed wooden gallery of Stick-style design which appears to have been painted to match the red and white masonry.[12]

Color schemes B and C present less dramatic alternatives, but ones which suggest the contrasting richness appropriate to a house of similar character and period.

	Scheme A	Scheme B	Scheme C
Paint Line	COOK AND DUNN/HISTORIC	CALIFORNIA/PURITAN VILLAGE	COOK AND DUNN/HISTORIC
Body	Somerset Gray	Manchester Gray 45061	Limestone
Stick Trim	Cranberry	Dove Gray 45051	Bottle Green 281
Sash	Cranberry	Manchester Gray 45061	Bottle Green 281
Door	frame— Cranberry panels— Somerset Gray	frame— Dove Gray 45051 panels— Manchester Gray 45061	frame— Bottle Green 281 panels— Limestone

Consult the Directory of Suppliers, pp. 117-118, for complete manufacturers' names, product lines, and addresses.

27. *Stockton Cottage, 1871-72*

AMERICAN RESORT ARCHITECTURE has often been more fanciful and playful than its counterpart "at home." This seems as true of the great marble summer "cottages" of Newport as it does of the quaint little bungalows constructed by the working classes along the crowded streets of seaside oases. The result of many factors, not least of which were the rise in popularity of the seaside vacation and the exuberant nineteenth-century architectural styles, houses located in resort locations seem to suggest the lighter side of Victorian life.

Apart from the most fashionable resorts, including Newport, Saratoga Springs, and Elberon, New Jersey, where the wealthy "watered" and strolled, the seaside settings where the majority of Americans spent their leisure time help to explain a few of the major currents in American life during the late 1800s. Of the country's many seaside resorts, one of the most illustrative of playful architecture within a typically rigid setting is Oak Bluffs, the Methodist campground on Martha's Vineyard. With a history of religious affiliation dating back to 1835, Oak Bluffs was among the preeminent Methodist campgrounds in late nineteenth-century America, so much so that by 1874 President and Mrs. Grant made a celebrated visit to the so-called "Cottage City of America."[1]

The clearest image of Oak Bluff's character and appearance before the turn of the century is best seen in a collection of old photographs now owned by the Dukes County Historical Society. Beyond the architectural clues they provide are fascinating portraits of often dour-faced families sitting before fancifully painted cottages upon which were sometimes hung printed messages proclaiming the ill effects of "demon rum."[2] These cottages, said to have been directly inspired by earlier canvas-covered wooden–frame tents, are, like their antecedents, set on wooden platforms which served as gathering porches for the inhabitants. Along with generous window openings framed by large and generally open shutters, uncovered porches give a hint of the friendly, open-spirited atmosphere that seems to have been the norm at places such as Oak Bluffs—and Ocean Grove—as long as one was temperate. With a population that reportedly surged to upwards of 30,000 on mid-summer weekends, Oak Bluffs attracted not only the religious visitor, but also those who came just to look at the gaily painted cottages set among the island's native oak.

The Stockton Cottage illustrated here was built far south of Oak Bluffs in 1872 and still stands in the oceanfront community of Cape May, New Jersey. Though not of an architectural form inspired by the early wooden-frame tent, the Stockton Cottage, one of a number of identical houses built in a row, has several similarities with the Oak Bluff cottages. Despite its larger size, one of its most interesting shared features is its platform-like base, a feature seldom seen in more urban locations where a basement generally elevated the first floor of a house three or four feet above the finished grade. Both house types also share a very conscious use of highly decorative cutwork trim, exemplifying the light-hearted nature of Victorian seaside life. In addition, the Stockton Cottage, like many of its Oak Bluffs counterparts, has an open, beckoning porch at ground level and a roofless galleried deck directly above, which is more suggestive of a stage or viewing platform than many of those examples found on year-round residences.

The color selection illustrated may be surprising, but is intended to suggest a scheme appropriate to a house located in a resort setting. Though it is impossible to ascertain the colors used on the Oak Bluff houses without microscopic analyses of extant sheathing, examinations of photographs clearly indicate that they were painted in a variety of contrasting colors and that the highlighting or "picking-out" of certain details was common. Window sash was often painted a dark color, as were exterior shutters; cutwork and bargeboards were frequently painted in what appears to have been white or very light colors not unlike lacework, perhaps the effect being sought. Wooden roofs, often in varieties of shapes, were frequently painted in two colors placed in horizontal bands, a treatment that accentuated the shingle patterns.

The color shown on the Stockton Cottage, was a shade familiar to nineteenth-century homeowners. Often applied over brickwork or as a trim or sash color, it was frequently suggested for use on a Queen Ann-style house where it was combined with browns and ambers among the strapwork and cut shingles to help emphasize the variety of architectural detailing.[4] On this example, the color choice seems especially suited to the setting. Two alternate schemes are also included.

	Scheme A	Scheme B	Scheme C
Paint Line	COOK AND DUNN/HISTORIC	COOK AND DUNN	CALIFORNIA/PURITAN VILLAGE
Body	Cape Russet	Plymouth Sage	Barn Red 45081
Trim #1	cornerboards, posts— Sandstone	cornerboards, posts— Concord Green 257	cornerboards, posts— Forest Green 47125
Trim #2	cutwork— Cottage Beige	trim #2 Forest Moss	trim #2 Forest Green 47125
Sash	Ashford Blue	Exterior Bottle Green	Weston Green 45076
Shutters	frames— Jersey Clay insets— Cape Russet	Exterior Bottle Green 281	frames— Forest Green 47125 insets— Weston Green 45076
Door	panels— Jersey Clay frame—Cape Russet	grained	grained

Consult the Directory of Suppliers, pp. 117-118, for complete manufacturers' names, product lines, and addresses.

Stockton Cottage, Cape May, New Jersey

1091 Harrison Street, Santa Clara, California

28. 1091 Harrison Street, c. 1890

CONCURRENT WITH THE DEVELOPMENT of the American preservation movement over the last decade or so has been the growth of interest in late-nineteenth-century architecture and decorative arts. Due in part to an oversaturation of information on the eighteenth century, the rediscovery of the late-Victorian past seems especially timely as the end of the twentieth century draws closer. In the forefront of renewed interest in the era is the Historic American Buildings Survey which, during the past several years, has surveyed significant buildings from the late 1800s. The house illustrated—1091 Harrison Street, Santa Clara, California—is but one example of the agency's most recent survey work. One of seven individual houses along Harrison Street, this building and its neighbors represent an important extant period streetscape of modest yet well detailed residences built for a prosperous middle class. The Harrison Street complex, said to have been one of Santa Clara's finest blocks at the turn of the century, displays a typical eclectic assemblage of Queen Anne, Stick, and Shingle-style architectural forms.[1] As the HABS survey-

ors have pointed out, part of the importance of this domestic grouping lies in the display of exuberant millwork and the dependence on pattern book designs of the 1890s. In addition, this group of structures provides what is becoming an increasingly rare glimpse of the late-nineteenth-century domestic streetscape unspoiled by modernized porches and picture windows.

As research and even common sense suggest, simple, smaller-scaled houses like these in Santa Clara and across America were generally painted only one body color. Many contemporary photographs support this finding and often show similarly sized houses painted in a very light body color—possibly white—with a minimum amount of contrasting trimwork. To be sure, painting a house during the 1800s was, as it still is today, an expensive procedure. It, therefore, seems logical to imagine that those of modest means would have favored less vigorous and costly paint schemes. Beyond that, it seems clear that white remained a popular exterior color for domestic use despite the years of A. J. Downing's influence and the urgings to the contrary of

the ever increasing number of paint companies.

Several years ago, while rummaging through a stock of old photographs in a San Francisco second-hand shop, I came across an old view of a two-story late-nineteenth-century frame house not unlike some of those built along Harrison Street. Possibly taken in Stockton, California, where the photographer's studio was located, the picture offers a number of period details of special importance to the preservationist. Among the most interesting is the color scheme. The house appears to have been painted white, with only its window sash, exterior shutters, screen door, basement skirting, and front steps painted in a contrasting color. Though the color applied to the sash, shutters, and screen door is impossible to determine, it appears as if these were all painted in the same color, possibly a light shade of gray, a common porch floor and step color.

In spite of indications that white was a more commonly occurring body color than previously suspected—especially in certain regions—the three color schemes for this house type are consistent with a more vibrant late-nineteenth-century palette.[2] Color scheme A is inspired by the colors shown on a house depicted in a "mourning picture" painted in 1889. Though the house shown in the painting by Edwin Romanzo Elmer is in the Italianate style, it is painted a color that became popular during the 1880s. Elmer, who painted this family portrait to memorialize his daughter

Effie, who had died at the age of eight, portrays his handsome house with a body of medium olive green, darker olive trim, and decorative detailing "picked-out" in what seems to have been a very light gray and an Indian red. The front door and the base of the porch columns are shown in brown, the former probably painted and grained in the usual fashion. An interesting interior feature which contributes to a unified scheme are the wooden inside shutters which seem to have been made of a stained blond-colored wood.[3]

Color scheme B suggests yet another typical monochromatic exterior treatment suitable when numerous colors would be ill-advised on such a small-scale house. Scheme C, not surprisingly, presents an option for a white-colored scheme and has been inspired by that on the little Queen Anne house shown in the old photograph mentioned previously.

	Scheme A	Scheme B	Scheme C
Paint Line	PITTSBURGH/HISTORIC	COOK AND DUNN/HISTORIC	CALIFORNIA/PURITAN VILLAGE
Body	Pony Express 4335	Somerset Gray	Colony White 47144
Trim	Soldier Green 4342	Somerset Gray	Colony White 47144
Sash	Colony Red 4187	Bottle Green 281	Winchester Gray 47150
Shutters	if used— Soldier Green 4342	if used— Bottle Green 281	if used— Winchester Gray 47150
Door	(natural finish)	(natural finish)	(natural finish) or Winchester Gray 47150

Consult the Directory of Suppliers, pp. 117-118, for complete manufacturers' names, product lines, and addresses.

The John McConnell House, Cape May, New Jersey

AFTER YEARS OF nationalistic concern about establishing a peculiarly American architectural form, a style with definite British origins took firm hold in this country during the last two decades of the nineteenth century. This style, known as the Queen Anne, flourished in an era of growing prosperity. The style's rich and complex profile was most appreciated as the very epitome of material success. A tangible architectural expression of this Gilded Age, the Queen Anne house, largely a composition of brick and wood, also employed various combinations of shingles, decorative terra-cotta tiles, stone, and stained glass to accentuate the material richness and texture of the completed structure. The technique was often so deft that surviving examples are as fresh and vibrant today as when first conceived.

The name of the style is actually a misnomer and refers to the mistaken notion that Anne was queen during the time when classical architectural forms began to appear on late medieval-style buildings.[1] The combination of half-timbering and classically-inspired detailing, therefore, that most Americans think of as a Queen Anne house, bears a singularly inappropriate name.[2] Nonetheless, the name held—and probably rightfully so, for houses of this type have a certain graciousness and majesty that well suggest the dignity generally ascribed to monarchy. No less true of its interior arrangements, a Queen Anne house most often implies a comfortable position in society, an almost ceremonial way of life well-exemplified by the style's gradually

29. The John McConnell House, 1883

ascending principal staircase within a large central "living hall." Though often associated with a large suburban mansion set within well-tended grounds, the style was easily adapted to smaller dwellings, not unlike the one illustrated. Many of these more modest houses can still be found along suburban streets across the country.

The Queen Anne style was popularized in America through the published works of British architects, most notably that of Richard Norman Shaw (1831-1912). In this country well-known architects, including McKim, Mead and White, H. H. Richardson, Bruce Price, and Wilson Eyre, contributed such elements from the American architectural tradition as wood framing and various colonial-inspired forms to give a decided eclectic feeling to the Americanized style.[3]

It is not surprising that an architecture of such textural richness and general complexity of form was also an architecture in which color played a significant role. Illustrative of this fact are Queen Anne build-

	Scheme A	Scheme B	Scheme C
Paint Line	COOK AND DUNN/HISTORIC	COOK AND DUNN/EXTERIOR	CALIFORNIA/PURITAN VILLAGE
Body ©1	Cranberry	Forest Moss	Manchester Gray 45061
Body ©2	Concord Green 257	Virginia Gold	*
Body ©3	Moss	Plymouth Sage	*
Trim	Cranberry	Colonial Red 280	Dove Gray 45051
Sash	Pewter	Bottle Green 281	Black 47102
Other			*On this scheme only one body color is used.

Consult the Directory of Suppliers, pp. 117-118, for complete manufacturers' names, product lines, and addresses.

ings solely of masonry. In many of these examples, combinations of several differently colored bricks, mortars, terra-cotta embellishments, tiles, and quarried stones present as varied a color palette as painted wooden counterparts on frame houses.

Some believe that Queen Anne houses were so variously and colorfully painted because the fast-developing paint industry encouraged the practice. While such reasoning might justify the widening availability of a variety of colors, it is shortsighted given the architectural palette itself and the broader influences which were at work. First, the stylistic form and the materials used to express it emphasized texture and rich, natural colors. Secondly, by the time the Queen Anne style emerged in the 1880s, a very strong tradition of color use stressing natural tints had been established. Downing's proscription against the use of white in favor of more naturally-inspired colors was widely disseminated. Thirdly, the all-pervasive mood of the entire post-Civil War period, a time that Lewis Mumford has called "The Brown Decades," was characterized by an artistic preoccupation with browns, russets, and ochres, colors which dominated some of the works of its most sympathetic artists.[4]

The John McConnell House is a fine example of a modestly scaled Queen Anne house. Built in Cape May, New Jersey, in 1883, the house is shown restored to its original appearance before minor alterations were made. The color scheme recognizes the three-part architectural composition of the building—a base or first story, a middle or second story, and a gable or third-floor area. According to the practice of the time, and most logically, the base has been painted with the darkest or "heaviest" of the three major colors. Accordingly, the two remaining levels have been painted with the medium color on the second level and the lightest color at the top. Window sash has been shown the same color at all levels and is, in this case, a limestone shade. The decorative strapwork, recalling British medieval influence, has been painted the same dark color as the base color since it implies a structural component. In this manner, the stronger color of the base effectively "holds the house together" and acts as the unifier for the entire composition.[5]

Two alternate color schemes are also included in the chart. Color scheme B suggests a three-part color scheme. Color scheme C is a more conservative composition not uncommon in its time.[6] Still recognizing the textual subtleties of the building's materials, C suggests a less costly and more easily maintainable alternative, but one which is as authentic as the first two suggestions.

30. The Middlecoff-Baier House, c. 1890

THE HANDSOME RED BRICK house shown in this section is representative of a stylish and solid upper-middle-class residence of the late nineteenth century. Located in Paxton, Illinois, the house was built during the early 1890s by the founder of a local brick and tile company, a fact which likely accounts for the gables being covered in slate to match the roof, rather than with the more commonly seen cut and patterned wooden shingles.

Like so many of its contemporaries, the Middlecoff-Baier House is a typical combination of styles and forms which make it impossible to precisely categorize. Of a general Queen Anne character, perhaps best exemplified by its picturesque profile, the house displays the rich texture, classically inspired detailing, and complex forms that are among the hallmarks of that style. At the same time, the building is vaguely reminiscent of the Romanesque idiom, as popularized by the architect H. H. Richardson. The solid nature of the building, imparted by the choice of building materials, the large and undivided expanses of glass, and the general robustness of the building's overall character, indicates at least an awareness of the second style. Indeed, the Middlecoff-Baier House, like so many others of its period, is truly eclectic, borrowing elements from the most fashionable styles and creating a house of strong character and solidity so characteristic of the era in which it was built.

The color scheme for such a dwelling should be largely determined by the color and texture of the brick used as facing. Varying according to manufacture and location of origin, brick could be laid with various mortar colors as well as with a variety of joints, elements which impart an overall tone to the face of a wall.[1] Information concerning the original paint scheme of the Middlecoff-Baier House exists in a brief notation attached to the drawings which were produced when the house was recorded by HABS in 1981: "the wood trim was originally painted a dark green." With that as a clue, the illustration shows a green not unlike that which is known to have been popular at the time and which, in fact, is still used in certain locales as the trim color on brick houses of this period.[2] In addition, and consistent with a common nineteenth-century procedure, the window

The Middlecoff-Baier House, Paxton, Illinois

sash has been closely colored to approximate the color of the bricks themselves. This treatment reinforces the feeling of the solidity and strength of the wall surface, and, complemented by the dark green trim, creates a tension between the structural and decorative elements of the house.[3]

Alternate schemes for a brick house of this style should generally be selected according to the color of the masonry. Color scheme B, which assumes a brick of the same color as shown, indicates that both sash and trim have been painted brown, a shade reminiscent of brownstone and consistent with the fact that, in many instances, stone trim was used in combination with red brick. Scheme C, which also assumes a red brick façade, recommends an olive green for the sash, with a slightly darker shade for the remaining woodwork. An additional scheme, though not listed, could include a medium gray tone as a sash color and the green shown in the illustration as the trim color. The use of white as either a sash or trim color should not be considered.

	Scheme A	Scheme B	Scheme C
Paint Line	BENJAMIN MOORE/HIGH GLOSS	GLIDDEN/HISTORIC	BENJAMIN MOORE/HIGH GLOSS
Body	red brick	red brick	red brick
Trim	Park Green 40	Bedford Road 15554	Park Green 40
Sash	Cottage Red 22	Winthrope 21793	Tate Olive HC-112
Shutters	if used— Chrome Green 41	if used— Sleepy Hollow 42774	if used— Park Green 40
Door	(natural finish)	(natural finish)	(natural finish)

Consult the Directory of Suppliers, pp. 117-118, for complete manufacturers' names, product lines, and addresses.

31. The John R. Halliday House, 1905

THE MODEST STORY-AND-A-HALF brick house built in 1905 for John R. Halliday is a good example of the adaptability of various late-nineteenth-century architectural styles to the smaller, domestic structure. Built in Pleasant Grove, Utah, a small town about thirty miles south of Salt Lake City, the Halliday House typifies the interest in and popularity of so-called "high style" architecture in areas well away from larger, more urban regions. The skills of the mason, carpenter, and glass artisan are clearly evident, as is the builder's knowledge of architectural styles and their adaptability to both the needs of a client and to the setting.

The most characteristic features of Halliday's house are the brick walls, accented with molded bricks at the window heads; the combinations of fenestration; and the asymmetric composition neatly contained beneath a complexity of hipped roofs. Of an overall Queen Anne style, of which all these features are characteristic, the little house is boldly punctuated by prominent chimneys which define the building's self-assured place within its community. As was common when eclecticism was almost a "style" in itself, the house also displays elements of the solid Romanesque idiom generally associated with structures of a far larger size.[1] It is tempting to speculate that, in using a few elements of the Romanesque, Halliday may have been subtly suggesting his prominent social position as founder of the local bank. The round-headed windows and the so-called eyebrow dormer in the roof are, of course, prominent features of the Romanesque.

Perhaps owing to its date of construction, elements of the Colonial Revival style can also be seen. The rather elegant front porch and entry portico with its Doric columns and applied neoclassical decoration of wreaths and garlands lend an air of refinement that appealed to many socially aspiring Americans of the day. The handsome wooden cornice, a further neoclassical reference, coexists quite comfortably with Queen Anne and Romanesque features, a situation not uncharacteristic of the more provincial compositions of the period.

The color scheme chosen for the Halliday House suggests one that would have been popular during the time the residence was built. A "Colonial" house, which may have been the way the house was originally described, is seen to best advantage when "done-up" in Colonial Revival colors. The deep, rich, and luxuriant tints of the high-Queen Anne style, such as those shown on the McConnell House (chapter 29), are not as effective on a building such as Halliday's. Colonial Revival colors include ivories and whites, grays, yellows, creams, and blues and greens—all colors then thought to have been a part of the palette of the 1700s.[2] Generally characteristic of the color use was the application of only one body color instead of the two or more which had been seen only a few years before. On the Halliday House, the brick is shown as painted.

A second color scheme could authentically follow that suggested for the Middlecoff-Baier House (chapter 30) except that in this instance the brick façade would be painted to imitate a redder brick.

A third scheme suggests that the natural brick be left unpainted. The color chosen for trim and sash would therefore need to be carefully selected to complement the color of the brick. White trim and sash would be inappropriate in this instance.

	Scheme A	Scheme B	Scheme C
Paint Line	—	BENJAMIN MOORE	CALIFORNIA/PURITAN VILLAGE
Body	California/Newport Langley Grey	High Gloss Clapboard Buff	Old Colonial 45087
Trim	California/Puritan Village White 28800	High Gloss Tate Olive HC-112	Colony White 47144
Sash	California/Puritan Village White 28800	Historic Pittsfield Buff HC-24	Colony White 47144
Shutters	if used— Cook and Dunn/Historic Pewter	if used— High Gloss Essex Green 43	if used— Black 47102 or Forest Green 47125
Door	(natural finish)	(natural finish)	(natural finish)

Consult the Directory of Suppliers, pp. 117-118, for complete manufacturers' names, product lines, and addresses.

The John R. Halliday House, Pleasant Grove, Utah

The George W. Boyd House, Cape May, New Jersey

32. The George W. Boyd House, 1911

As with other American revival styles, it is difficult to specify precisely when a resurgence of interest in colonial-inspired architectural forms began to be reflected in domestic buildings. While the colonial-, or more precisely, Georgian-inspired symmetrical house had never really disappeared from the American scene, only the form and pattern of the style, rather than specific details, continued to be followed. Dressed in a succession of popular styles throughout the 1800s, the form was successfully labeled Greek Revival, Gothic Revival, Italianate and several other styles, while maintaining its basic Georgian-inspired exterior form and interior plan.

	Scheme A	Scheme B	Scheme C
Paint Line	CALIFORNIA/PURITAN VILLAGE	BENJAMIN MOORE/ HIGH GLOSS	BENJAMIN MOORE
Body	Sun Yellow 21887	Briarwood 73	High Gloss English Ivory 17
Trim	Colony White 47144	Navajo White 72	High Gloss Navajo White 72
Sash	Colony White 47144	Navajo White 72	MoorGard and MoorGlo Black 80
Shutters	Forest Green 47125	Park Green 40	MoorGard and MoorGlo Black 80
Door	Forest Green 47125	Park Green 40	MoorGard and Moor Glo Black 80
Other		alternate sash color— Park Green 40	alternate sash color — High Gloss Navajo White 72

Consult the Directory of Suppliers, pp. 117-118, for complete manufacturers' names, product lines, and addresses.

Not until the third quarter of the nineteenth century did the buildings themselves begin consciously to assume the character and detailing of the Colonial and Neoclassical buildings of the eighteenth and early nineteenth centuries. By 1876, when the centennial of the signing of the Declaration of Independence was celebrated, the stage was set for a nostalgic and characteristically romantic return to the country's cultural heritage.

Several young and soon-to-be-prominent architects expressed great interest in the American architectural past. During the 1870s a growth of interest in seaside vacations brought attention to the relatively unspoiled colonial coastal towns of Newport, Portsmouth, and Marblehead—all within easy travel of Boston and all with major examples of Colonial and Federal architecture. Appealing to wealthy Bostonians and New Yorkers, these towns also attracted their architects, several of whom developed lifelong preoccupations with the architectural forms, details, and decorative elements of eighteenth-century structures. Such architects as Charles F. McKim (who as early as 1872 "restored" rooms in an eighteenth-century Newport house), Arthur Little, and Bruce Price, among others, took inspiration from the historic patrimony in creating some of the architectural masterpieces of their own age.[1]

The Colonial Revival domestic form was significantly different from the architecture which inspired it. In most every instance, the Colonial Revival house of the late 1800s was an architecture of exaggeration. True to the spirit of its time, the average revival house was invariably an eclectic mixture of period-inspired elements and might include such disparate elements as a Palladian window placed in an attic gable, a Mount Vernon-style colonnade, the gambrel roof of a New England sea captain's house, stained glass, a porte-cochère, and bow windows. Of generally large scale, the Colonial Revival house was clearly a stylistic phenomenon made possible by other grandiose Victorian styles, the personal wealth of clients, the availability of skilled craftsmen, and the architectural background of those who pioneered the style, many of whom were trained in the grand manner of the École des Beaux Arts. Despite the often overbearing nature and the exaggerated detailing of these buildings, many are nonetheless charming and well-crafted representations of an earlier period of American architectural history.

The George W. Boyd House, illustrated here, is an example of a Georgian Colonial-Revival domestic structure of the early twentieth century. Characteristically restrained and more accurately detailed than its late-nineteenth-century counterparts, the Boyd House is, despite its high platform, more comfortably scaled than similar houses constructed a quarter-century before. Obviously designed to address the climate and seaside location, the Boyd House, built in Cape May, New Jersey, in 1911, shows the well-studied academic influence of such important firms as McKim,

Mead and White that were simultaneously designing houses of similar chasteness and "simplicity" for clients along the eastern seaboard.

Colonial Revival color schemes were, quite logically, inspired by the colors then believed to be those used by early Americans. Yellow was among the most popular. One of the greatest of all Colonial Revival houses, that built for H.A.C. Taylor in 1885, was painted yellow, and is the inspiration for color scheme A. Designed by McKim, Mead and White and built in Newport, Rhode Island, the house was to be of a color inspired by "an old fashioned" local residence.[2] Several contemporary photographs of the house indicate that the trim was painted white and the window sash a very dark color—possibly dark green.[3] Without doubt, the architects were instrumental in the color selection.

Color scheme B recommends medium gray for the body, with white trim and black shutters; scheme C specifies an ivory body color with black shutters. Other appropriate Colonial Revival color schemes for houses of similar size would include body colors of beige or tan, green, or blue—each with white trim. Of course, a scheme with a white body and green shutters would also be appropriate.

The Saratoga Foothills Club, Saratoga, California

In RESPONSE TO burgeoning industrial development and the subsequent need for inexpensive housing, many early twentieth-century families made use of books offering plans for small homes which could be erected at moderate cost in affordable areas away from the city center. Designed largely for young middle-class couples with more progressive ideas and informal life styles than their parents, these "bungalows," as they were somtimes called, responded to the owners' needs in ways that the architecture of the previous century had not.[1]

Among the most popular and widely circulated of the printed materials offering ideas, plans, and drawings was *The Craftsman,* a magazine published between 1901 and 1916 that featured simple, modestly scaled houses. Gustav Stickley, the originator and publisher best remembered today for his furniture, favored buildings built of natural materials that would fit well into a natural setting. In a tone reminiscent of Orson Squire Fowler who had extolled the economy of the octagonal house only a half-century before,[2] Stickley wrote that his Craftsman house was economical and easy to construct because it could be built by local craftsmen from local materials.[3]

Though there were large-scale Craftsman-style houses, the largest numbers were modestly scaled bungalows usually a story-and-a-half in height. Influenced in large measure by the superbly crafted work of the California architects Greene and Greene, these American or California bungalows, as they were sometimes called, varied according to local conditions,

33. The Saratoga Foothills Club, 1915

climate, and customs, though several characteristics are common to most. Wood or concrete—and often stucco—were favored for the exteriors, and frequently brick of a rough or even molten texture was used for accent. Porches and terraces, especially in California examples, were common as were large areas of glass and an interior arrangement of surprising openness in which rooms flowed easily together.

Low-pitched roofs and exposed structural members, most often roof joists, were additional features which characterized the style.[4]

The pleasant building illustrated here was designed by the architect Julia Morgan (1872-1957) and is one of a number of buildings designed by her in the Craftsman style as women's clubs.[5] The southwest elevation shown is really the garden side of

	Scheme A	Scheme B	Scheme C
Paint Line	COOK AND DUNN	GLIDDEN/HISTORIC	MURALO/ULTIMATE
Body	Exterior Plymouth Sage	Cromwell 25592	Burlap 34C-2T
Trim	Historic Sandstone	Chandlery 21783	India 21B-4D
Sash	Historic Sandstone	Bedford Road 15554	India 21B-4D
Shutters	—	—	—
Door	Historic Sandstone	Chandlery 21783	Tudor Brown 61
Other	roof— stained brown	roof— stained brown	roof— stained medium-brown

Consult the Directory of Suppliers, pp. 117-118, for complete manufacturers' names, product lines, and addresses.

the building and was chosen for illustration both because of its domestic character and for the manner in which it exemplifies the style. As is true of Morgan's work, the building is sophisticated, well detailed, and beautifully proportioned while maintaining the elegant simplicity that is perhaps one of the true marks of architectural genius. It strikes, moreover, an interesting contrast with her better-known work at San Simeon, the extravagant hilltop estate of William Randolph Hearst upon which she spent so many years of work.

The Saratoga Foothills Club, located near San Francisco, was completed in 1915 at a cost of about $5,000.[6] One of the most important points about the building is its careful relation to its well-landscaped site. A pergola, leading to the doorway, covers a walkway at the garden's edge. The placement of large windows with lowered sills and a construction of redwood—with a natural stain—are consistent with the ideals that the Craftsman style reflected.

The writings of Stickley are very instructive concerning popular exterior colors for houses in this style. Among the most frequently mentioned in *The Craftsman* are colors that he termed natural gray, dull green, warm green, biscuit, moss green, and brown, the latter two of which were

sometimes wood stains. These shades were often used in combination with naturally colored materials such as tapestry bricks which ranged in hue from dark red, gray green, dark gold, and dark maroon, as well as with boulders and fieldstones. In certain locations, bricks of a very molten appearance with iridescent glazes are also seen and are laid in irregular courses, presenting a rough and natural texture well-favored by the style's proponents.[7]

Exterior walls of wooden construction were sometimes left in their natural state with only a preservative coating or wood stain applied across the surface. Roofs, if not of wooden shakes or shingles, were sometimes tiled, especially in those instances where attempts were made to evoke a Spanish flavor in the overall architectural composition. Porch floors, at least in many of Stickley's illustrated examples, were often of concrete scored into squares and painted red. Still others were covered with terra-cotta tiles.[8]

Each of the recommended color schemes has been derived from examples discussed in Stickley's publications. Scheme A indicates a body of moss green rather than the naturally stained redwood which was—and remains—the exterior scheme on the Saratoga Foothills Club.

34. 1090 and 1092 O'Brien Court, 1920s

SUITABLY DESIGNED TO complement the region in which they were built, houses such as these "Spanish-style" bungalows in San Jose, California, are as much a part of the architectural heritage of their area as the many "Cape Cods" which pepper the Northeast. Built during the 1920s as part of a speculative venture, these little houses were priced between $5,500 and $6,500, making them affordable to young white-collar and skilled factory workers.[1]

The categorization of many of the examples of American buildings into specific stylistic headings is far from an exact science. While the houses illustrated here, for example, are clearly derivative of a particular historical period—namely the Spanish Mission—they are no exception to this indexing dilemma since their "architecture" is both applied and eclectic. In addition, some of the other houses along O'Brien Court, built as part of the same speculative venture presumably by the same builder, are less of the "Mission style" than what might be termed the "Spanish Fort style" and which some have called "Pueblo Revival."[2] That some of these houses have

English cottage windows with diamond-shaped panes confuses the issue still further. And, of course, since individual builders interpreted the general style in their own fashion, any categorizing is made even more difficult. The visual variety is in itself an important indicator of the general popularity of home ownership and of individual architectural expression. It also reflects the interest voiced by the popular architectural theorist of the early 1900s, Gustav Stickley, in providing Americans with simple, attractive, and easily built dwellings.[3]

In *The Craftsman* of January, 1904, Stickley provided a design for a house in the so-called "California Mission Style." Its architectural elements, consisting of simple cement-struccoed walls, round arched openings, and tile roofs, are similar to elements seen at 1092 O'Brien Court, although Stickley's house is much larger. Stickley, naturally, was interested in the exterior color schemes of the houses he illustrated. In writing about the California house, he noted that three elements were important in assuring the success of its

1090 and 1092 O'Brien Court, San Jose, California

façade—the use of simple building materials, the use of decoration only as a product of structure, and the relation between the building's setting and its exterior color.[4]

Noting the warm, natural color palette of California and the South, Stickley suggested a color scheme of cream-colored biscuit for the house's walls and a roof of dull red tiles. In northern or colder climates, he recommended that the same house be painted a natural gray—actually the color of the unpainted cement walls—or a dull green, which he suggested could be unevenly applied across the stuccoed surface to produce an unusual effect.[5]

The color schemes shown employ colors that Stickley would approve since the buildings are located in an environment suitable to warm, creamy shades. For the body of number 1090 a pale orange-tan, suggesting the warm tones of unpainted adobe, is recommended. The window sash and door are painted brown. As in many houses illustrated by Stickley, the tile roof is a dull red as is the porch flooring, which according to several of his notations was often concrete scored to look like clay tile.[6]

Color scheme B, shown on 1092 O'Brien Court, is of the ubiquitous white, a color apparently not popular with Stickley, but one with a long history of use in areas of warm climate and bright sunlight. In this instance, the sash has been painted a dark gray, a color favored by Stickley and probably achieved with a wood stain rather than with paint.[7]

Color scheme C, not shown, is a rather somber treatment suggesting a setting in a colder climate where, incidentally, houses in this style were sometimes built. A natural gray, somewhat the color of unpainted concrete, is highlighted with trim and sash of dark gray. The roof, which might in some instances be sheathed in flat tiles, slates, or wood, was suggested by Stickley to be either gray or of soft moss green. In recommending this color scheme, he also advised the addition of white painted columns.

The exterior color treatment of the detached garage, which came to be an important addition to houses during the 1920s, should be noted. Many of these are still extant. The best and most authentic treatment is simply to paint the walls the body color of the house and to paint the sash—if they exist—either white or the sash color of the house. The doors and other decorative features such as wooden gables or louvered vents should be treated with caution lest the application of too much color on such a small structure detract from the house. Doors can be painted white or even gray to match a fence. Or, if original swing doors with panels or crossed stiles remain in place, they can be highlighted with the body color of the house. Modern overhead doors, however, should be painted the body color of the garage to minimize their unauthentic impact.

	1090 O'Brien Ct. Scheme A	1092 O'Brien Ct. Scheme B	1090 or 1092 O'Brien Ct. Scheme C
Paint Line	MURALO/RESTORATION	—	—
Body	Copper Kettle 20C-3D	Benjamin Moore/High Gloss Navajo White 72	Pittsburgh/Historic Mission Gray 2756
Trim	Suede 36C-4A	Pittsburgh/Historic Old Silver 3757	Pittsburgh/Historic Old Silver 3757
Sash	Suede 36C-4A	Pittsburgh/Historic Old Silver 3757	Benjamin Moore/High Gloss Navajo White 72
Shutters	—	—	—
Door	Suede 36C-4A	Benjamin Moore/High Gloss Navajo White 72	Pittsburgh/Historic Old Silver 3757

Consult the Directory of Suppliers, pp. 117-118, for complete manufacturers' names, product lines, and addresses.

35. The Peter Col House, 1910

BUILDINGS IN THE STYLE of the Peter Col House most likely appear unusual to East Coast readers. To those living in the Midwest and on the West Coast, however, buildings of this character are less surprising since thousands of houses in the so-called "Prairie School" style were constructed after the turn of the century. At this time several young architects working in firms that were as adept at one style as with another reacted against the current eclecticism and concerned themselves with the development of an architecture more indicative of American life and aspirations. By the beginning of this century, the preeminent proponent of this architectural revolt was, of course, Frank Lloyd Wright who spent his life creating buildings that addressed "the issues" as had no other buildings previously constructed. The Peter Col House is clearly an example of a house designed by architects influenced by his work.

A product of the Midwestern spirit which at the time was perhaps fresher in its architectural approach than that of the East, Wright and his disciples began to design buildings that were wed to the landscape not only in profile but also in construction. The conscious effort to respond to the flat and gently rolling land was enhanced by the use of building materials indigenous or sympathetic to the natural character and colors of the locale. Low pitched roofs, or even flat ones, were pierced by chimneys intended, most often, to mark the symbolic center of the home around which most activity was centered. Windows, unlike so many on nineteenth-century houses located according to custom or for exterior effect, now began to define interior space and to direct natural light in ways that had not been done in the same manner before. Exterior finishes, very often of a stucco coating, were sometimes carried into the interior where the use of naturally treated wood, brick, and stone effectively unified the building. The impact of Wright's originality and his genius can hardly be underestimated.[1]

The Col House, built in San Jose, California, in 1910, is a good, modest example of the kind of building influenced by the Prairie School architects. Lacking the sophistication of Wright's hand, the building, like hundreds of others of similar design, reflects the high ideals of the architects and builders who constructed them. Unfortunately, the movement never developed to the extent that its early proponents had hoped, and it seems that most Americans decided that true domestic contentment could be experienced only within the walls of the traditional "colonials" that spread

	Scheme A	Scheme B	Scheme C
Paint Line	PITTSBURGH/HISTORIC	COOK AND DUNN/EXTERIOR	COOK AND DUNN/EXTERIOR
Body	Carlsbad Canyon 2606	Lexington Gray	Plymouth Sage
Trim	Fort Sill 7612	Navajo White	Quaker Brown
Sash	Fort Sill 7612	Forest Moss	Navajo White or Quaker Brown
Shutters	—	—	—
Door	Fort Sill 7612	Forest Moss	Quaker Brown or natural stain, medium brown

Consult the Directory of Suppliers, pp. 117-118, for complete manufacturers' names, product lines, and addresses.

The Peter Col House, San Jose, California

across the nation between the world wars.[2]

Designed by the firm of Wolfe and Wolfe, the Col House has been colored according to the precepts of Gustav Stickley expressed in *The Craftsman*.[3] In 1904 he illustrated "A Craftsman House Founded on The California Mission Style," noting the importance of color to the design. Stickley suggested as appropriate to California "a soft warm creamy tone, almost a biscuit color," topped by a roof of dull red.[4] As illustrated here, trim and sash have been painted dull red as well; this could easily be changed to a dull brown as an alternative. The concrete steps and terrace surface, as in many of Stickley's houses, have also been painted dull red, a color that Wright himself adapted in another variation as his own hallmark color and used to varying degrees in many of his buildings.

Color schemes B and C represent alternatives also derived from *The Craftsman*. Scheme B recommends a gray color often termed a "soft gray" by Stickley.[5] Scheme C, though perhaps less acceptable to our modern-day sensibility, is a period combination that could, depending on the architectural form of the house, be used to good effect. Stickley's scheme called for a dull-green body, brown trim, and accents of white for columns or posts, if present.[6] If a roof surface were visible, brown-stained wooden shingles would be appropriate. In certain warmer climates, white has traditionally been both an attractive body color and a practical one. Trim of a medium dull-brown shade would be an appropriate selection.

Proper mixing of commercial paint colors is a science that has been mastered by a number of American manufacturers. However, it is virtually impossible for a manufacturer to maintain a particular hue consistency over a long period of time. A color may even change from batch to batch or be altered for commercial reasons. In most cases, slight differences in shade are of little importance, but when attempting to re-create an authentic historic color scheme, every effort should be made to match a color as closely as possible. For this reason, each of the commercially available paint colors recommended in this book have been matched against the Munsell Color Notation System, which is the recognized standard coding system for color. The system, which does not deal with paint manufacture was developed early in the twentieth-century by Albert H. Munsell. The Munsell color code appears below opposite the commercial paint color. Where blank spaces appear after paint names, no close equivalent was found. The codes for black and white have also been omitted here, in most cases. The author wishes to thank Laney Loughridge and Edwin Stulb, Jr. of The Stulb Co./Allentown Paints for providing access to their copies of the Munsell Color System. The author wishes to thank Louise Galion of the Munsell Color System for assistance in checking the notational form. For further technical services, readers should contact The Munsell Color System, 2441 N. Calvert St., Baltimore, MD. 21218.

Chart of Standard Color Equivalents

Paint Color	Munsell Color Code
Benjamin Moore	
Black Briarwood 73	10YR 6/1
Chrome Green 41	10G 2/6
Clapboard Buff 55	2.5Y 8.5/4
Cliffside Gray 74	2.5R N8.5/
Colonial Yellow 10	2.5Y 8.5/6
Cottage Red 22	5R 3/6
English Ivory 17	2.5Y 9/4
Essex Green 43	10GY 2/2
Falcon Brown 1238	5YR 4/2
Garrison Red HC-66	7.5R 4/4

Paint Color	Munsell Color Code
Georgian Brick HC-50	10R 4/6
Greenfield Pumpkin HC-40	7.5YR 5/4
Hadley Red HC-65	
Hawthorne Yellow HC-4	5Y 9/4
Jamesboro Gold HC-88	2.5Y 6/4
Lancaster Whitewash HC-174	
Lynchburg Green 48	7.5GY 7/2
Navajo White 72	
Park Green 40	5G 3/6
Pittsfield Buff HC-24	2.5Y 9/2
Platinum Gray 71	N 7.5/
Sandpiper 59	10YR 7/2
Tate Olive HC-112	5GY 6/2
Thornwood White HC-27	
Tobacco Brown 61	5YR 4/4
California	
Antique White 28820	2.5Y 8.5/2
Arnold Green	5GY 5/2
Barn Red 45081	
Birchwood 45044	
Black 47102	
Chestnut Brown 47127	7.5Y 2/4
Colony House Gold	2.5Y 8.5/4
Colony White 47144	10YR 9/2
Document White 45082	10YR 9/2
Dove Gray 45051	5Y 6/1
Dudley Grey	5PB 6/2
Forest Green 47125	7.5G 2/4
Gilbert Stuart Brown	2.5YR 4/2
Manchester Gray 45061	
Nicholas Rose	7.5R 5/4

Paint Color	Munsell Color Code
Putnam Ivory 28835	2.5Y 9/2
Rockwell Red 28832	10R 3/6
Victorian Rose 45054	10R 6/4
Walnut Room Brown	2.5YR 4/4
Weston Green 45076	10GY 6/2
White 18800	
White Horse Tavern Red 47152	7.5R 4/4
Winchester Gray 47150	5PB 6/2
Cook and Dunn	
Academy Gray	5B 5/1
Amber Hall	5YR 6/8
Ashford Blue	5PB 6/4
Bisque	7.5YR 8/4
Black	
Bottle Green 281	7.5GY 2/2
Candlewhite	10YR 9/2
Cape Russet	2.5YR 5/8
Chestnut	10YR 6/6
Classic Ivory	10YR 9/1
Cobblestone	5YR 6/2
Colonial Red 280	5R 3/6
Colonial Yellow 259	10YR 8/6
Commons Green	7.5GY 5/2
Concord Green 257	7.5GY 3/2
Cottage Beige	10YR 8/2
Cranberry	2.5R 3/6
Essex	2.5Y 5/2
Forest Moss	5GY 6/1
Fort Mifflin Brown	
Gate Gray	5PB 5/1
Gothic Rose	5YR 8/2

Paint Color	Munsell Color Code
Jersey Buff	10YR 8/4
Jersey Clay	10R 5/6
Lamplight Cream	2.5Y 8.5/4
Lexington Gray	2.5R N6.5/
Limestone	10YR 7/2
Moss	7.5GY 4/2
Mullica	10Y 5/1
Parchment	5Y 8.5/1
Pewter	5B 6/1
Plymouth Sage	7.5Y 7/2
Quaker Brown	7.5YR 6/4
Sandstone	10YR 6/4
Smithtown Green	5GY 6/4
Somerset Gray	2.5R N8.5/
Taupewood	10YR 5/2
Tudor Brown	5YR 2/5
Tuscan Ivory	2.5Y 9/4
Virginia Gold	7.5YR 6/6

Finnaren and Haley

Paint Color	Munsell Color Code
Belmont Blue	10B 5/2
Black	
Brown	10R 3/1
Congress Hall Red	5R 4/4
Franklin White	2.5Y 9/2
Independence Hall White	2.5Y 8.5/2
Jamestown Red	5R 3/6
Lime White	2.5Y 8/2
Medium Green	7.5G 3/6
Monterey	2.5Y 9/2
Mt. Pleasant Pink	2.5YR 8/4
Pennfield Brown	5YR 3/2

Glidden

Paint Color	Munsell Color Code
Bedford Road 15554	10YR 5/4
Cambridge 18104	5Y 5/1
Chandlery 21783	2.5Y 6/4
Cromwell 25592	2.5Y 8/4
English Tudor 20984	5Y 4/1
Governor's Grove 30874	10Y 5/2
Oregon Trail 15783	10YR 6/4
Rushmore 27222	5Y 7/2
St. Michael's 21342	

Paint Color	Munsell Color Code
Sleepy Hollow 42774	2.5G 4/2
Tankard 41762	
Tarrytown 16503	2.5Y 8/4
Weathervane 75104	10B 4/1
Western Reserve 65333	10B 7/1
Winthrope 21793	5Y 8/2

Martin Senour/Williamsburg

Paint Color	Munsell Color Code
Benjamin Powell House Green	10GY 3/2
Bracken Tenement Biscuit W81-1064	10YR 8/4
Bracken Tenement Blue Slate W83-1065	10BG 4/1
James Moir Shop Fawn W82-1080	10YR 6/2
King's Arms Tavern Gray W83-1076	10YR 5/1
Nicholson Store Red W86-1081	10R 2/6
Peyton Randolph Gray W82-1086	5YR 6/1
William Byrd III House Ivory W81-1073	10YR 8/4

Muralo

Paint Color	Munsell Color Code
Burlap 34C-2T	7.5YR 7/4
Burgundy Dash 70A-1A	7.5R 4/6
Copper Kettle 20C-3D	5YR 6/6
Dark Green 363	10G 2/4
Hollyhock 51C-4D	7.5GY 6/4
India 21B-4D	2.5YR 5/6
Indian Tan 12C-24	5YR 7/2
Pewter Cup 13C-2T	N7.5/
Suede 36C-4A	7.5YR 5/4
Tudor Brown 61	2.5YR 3/2
Winter Sky 39A-2P	

Pittsburgh

Paint Color	Munsell Color Code
Carlsbad Canyon 2606	7.5YR 9/4
Colony Red 4187	10R 4/6
Fort Sill 7612	5YR 4/4
Hammered Iron 4760	5Y 5/1
Mission Gray 2756	5Y 8/1
Old Silver 3757	5Y 6/1
Pine Mountain 7336	5Y 3/4

Paint Color	Munsell Color Code
Soldier Green 4335	5Y 6/4
Springfield Rifle 7755	5Y 4/1

Pratt and Lambert

Paint Color	Munsell Color Code
Ballroom Tan 21 GV-P	2.5Y 8/2
Bayberry 23 GV-M	2.5Y 6/2
Carriage Green 8 GV-A	2.5Y 5/4
Eagle Tavern Gold 6 GV-M	2.5Y 7/6
Eagle Tavern Olive 15 GV-A	2.5B 4/2
Gallery Stripe Blue 35 GV-M	2.5B 6/2
Museum White 17 GV-W	
Pewter 28 GV-P	10YR 7/1
Pottery Brown 12 GV-A	7.5YR 5/4
Sarah Jordan Brown 11 GV-M	7.5 YR 6/4
Secretary House Green 14 GV-M	5GY 6/2
Secretary House Red 27 GV-A	7.5R 4/8
Stone Mill Gray 16 GV-A	10YR 5/1
Susquehanna Sand 10 GV-M	10YR 6/4
Veranda Gray 34 GV-P	
Wainscot Olive 24 GV-M	7.5Y 6/2
Webster Green 20 GV-A	5GY 3/1
Whitewash 9 GV-W	

Stulb (Old Village and Old Sturbridge Village)

Paint Color	Munsell Color Code
Antique Pewter	5Y 5/2
Antique Yellow	2.5Y 7/6
Cabinetmaker's Blue	2.5B 5/4
Colonial Green	5GY 5/2
Colonial White	
Fenno House Green 1114	7.5GY 4/2
Meeting House White 1101	
Sugar Box Green 1122	7.5GY 3/2
Town House Ivory 1123	10YR 6/4

Stulb (Breinig/Allentown)

Paint Color	Munsell Color Code
Cherry Red 10-567	10R 3/6
Dark Green 12-735	10G 2/4
Dawn Gray 10-478	N8.5/
Lead Color 10-494	N5.5/
Rich Straw 10-425	2.5Y 8.5/6

Directory of Suppliers of Historic Paint Colors

Manufacturers of exterior paints suitable for used on period dwellings are listed below. Nearly all of the firms are included in the recommended schemes for the thirty-five buildings illustrated. The various paint lines or collections are noted for each manufacturer. Some paints may not be available throughout the United States or Canada; the reader is advised to write for information and paint cards so that substitutions for recommended colors can be made if necessary.

ALLENTOWN PAINT Manufacturing Co., including Allentown, Breinig, and Pennsylvania Dutch lines (*see* Stulb)

BENJAMIN MOORE PAINTS
  High Gloss House Paint
  Historical Color Collection
  MoorGard and MoorGlo
51 Chestnut Ridge Rd.
Montvale, NJ 07645
(201) 573-9600

CABOT STAINS
Samuel Cabot, Inc.
1 Union St.
Boston, MA 02108
(617) 723-7740

CALIFORNIA PAINTS
  Historic Newport Colours
  Puritan Village Colour Portfolio
California Products Corp.
169 Waverly St.
Cambridge, MA 02139
(617) 547-5300

COOK AND DUNN
  Exterior Finishes
  Historic Colors
Cook and Dunn Paint Corp.
Box 117
Newark, NJ 07101
(201) 589-5580

FINNAREN AND HALEY PAINT
  Authentic Colors of Historic Philadelphia
  Exterior Colors Featuring Victorian Hues
Finnaren and Haley Paint
2320 Haverford Rd.
Ardmore, PA 19003
(215) 649-5000

GLIDDEN
  The American Color Legacy
The Glidden Co.
925 Euclid Ave.
Cleveland, OH 44115
(216) 835-7150

Martin-Senour Paints
Williamsburg Paint Colors
The Martin-Senour Co.
1370 Ontario Ave., NW
Cleveland, OH 44113
(216) 566-2316

Muralo
Exterior/Interior Historic Restoration Colors
Georgetown Low Luster Latex House Paint
Soft Gloss House and Trim Paint
Multimate MidGloss-Ultimate Flat
The Muralo Co., Inc.
148 E. 5th Ave.
Bayonne, NJ 07002
(201) 437-0770

Pittsburgh Paints
Historic Colors
Solid Color Stains
Pittsburgh Paints
One PPG Plaza
Pittsburgh, PA 15272
(412) 434-2400

Pratt and Lambert
Early Americana Colours from Henry Ford
Museum and Greenfield Village
Exterior Designer Colors
Pratt and Lambert
P.O. Box 22, Dept. GV
Buffalo, NY 14240
(716) 873-6000

Stulb
Allentown Paint
Breinig's House Paint
Old Village Paint Colors
Old Sturbridge Village Paint Colors
Pennsylvania Dutch
The Stulb Co.
618 W. Washington St.
Norristown, PA 19404
(215) 433-4273

Introduction

1. Painters had to be adept at a variety of procedures during an era when painting required much specialized preparation.
2. Richard M. Candee, conference address: "Paint in the American Colonies and Early Republic," Paint in America, A Symposium on Architectural and Decorative Paints, May 18, 1989.
3. Hezekiah Reynolds, *Directions for House and Ship Painting* (New Haven, 1812).
4. Richard M. Candee, "The Rediscovery of Milk-based House Paints and the Myth of 'Brick-dust and Buttermilk' Paints," *Old-Time New England*, p. 79.
5. Whitewash had wide use well into the twentieth century.
6. Theodore Zuk Penn, "Decorative and Protective Finishes, 1750-1850, Materials, Process and Craft, "*The Bulletin of the Association for Preservation Technology.* XVI, no. 1 (1984), p. 24.
7. Caroline Alderson, "Recreating a Nineteenth-Century Paint Palette," *The Bulletin of the Association for Preservation Technology.* XVI, no. 1 (1984), p. 47.
8. Penn, p. 24.
9. Ibid, pp. 3-23.
10. Ibid, pp. 7-10.
11. Ibid, p. 8.
12. Ibid.
13. Ibid, pp. 10-12.
14. Ibid, p. 11.
15. Ibid, p. 12.
16. Ibid, pp. 13-15.
17. Alderson, pp. 48-49.
18. Roger W. Moss and Gail Caskey Winkler, *Victorian Exterior Decoration, How to Paint Your Nineteenth-Century American House Historicaly* (New York: Henry Holt and Co., 1987), p. 20.
19. A reproduction of this card can be seen in Moss and Winkler, p. 21.
20. Moss and Winkler, pp. 22-31.
21. Ibid, p. 24.
22. For an example of these surprisingly "bright" colors, see Matthew John Mosca, "The House and Its Restoration," *The Magazine Antiques* (February, 1989), pp. 460-473.

Chapter 1

1. Brick buildings were often painted to refresh a façade or to bring an older building "up to fashion." Bricks were also painted as a means of preserving their often soft surfaces, especially as they aged.
2. Alan Gowans, *Images of American Living, Four Centuries of Architecture and Furniture as Cultural Expression* (Philadelphia: J. B. Lippincott Co., 1964), p. 142.

Notes

3. Hugh Morrison, *Early American Architecture, From the First Colonial Settlements to the National Period* (New York: Oxford University Press, 1952), p. 103.
4. Sarah Mytton Maury, *An Englishwoman in America* (Liverpool, 1848), pp. 163-164.
5. Morrisson, p. 106.
6. Roderic H. Blackburn, "Dutch Arts and Culture in Colonial America," *The Magazine Antiques* (July, 1986), pp. 140-151. The overmantel painting is shown and discussed in the article.
7. Morrison, pp. 115-116.

Chapter 2

1. Marcus Whiffen, *The Eighteenty-Century Houses of Williamsburg* (Williamsburg: Colonial Williamsburg, 1960), pp. 14-15.
2. Ibid.
3. Antoinette F. Downing and Vincent J. Scully, Jr., *The Architectural Heritage of Newport, Rhode Island* (New York: Bramhall House, 1967), p. 70.
4. Ibid, p. 69.
5. Ibid.
6. Theodore Zuk Penn, "Decorative and Protective Finishes, 1750-1850, Materials, Process, and Craft," *Bulletin of the Association for Preservation Technology*, XVI, no. 1 (1984), p. 13.
7. Whiffen, pp. 197-198.
8. Hezekiah Reynolds, *Directions for House and Ship Painting* (New Haven, 1812), p. 10. A facsimile of the book is reproduced in an article by Richard M. Candee, "Preparing and Mixing Colors in 1812," *The Magazine Antiques* (April, 1978), pp. 849-853.
9. Painting whereabouts unknown.
10. Whiffen, pp. 197-198.
11. Nicholas A. Pappas, FAIA, conference address: "Case Study: Paint Analysis and Interpretation at Colonial Williamsburg," Paint in America, A Symposium on Architectural and Decorative Paints, May 18, 1989.

Chapter 3

1. Matthew John Mosca, "The House and Its Restoration," *The Magazine Antiques* (February, 1989), pp. 463. Mosca writes about the recreation of Washington's vibrant interior paint selections at Mount Vernon.

2. William H. Pierson, Jr., *American Buildings and Their Architects, The Colonial and Neoclassical Styles* (New York: Anchor Press/Doubleday, 1976), p. 94.

3. A good example of this form can be seen on the extant Old Manse (c. 1768) in Deerfield, Massachusetts. A photograph and brief discussion of the house can be found in Pierson, *American Buildings,* pp. 88-90.

4. Antoinette F. Downing and Vincent J. Scully, Jr., *The Architectural Heritage of Newport, Rhode Island* (New York: Bramhall House, 1967), pp. 40, 67.

5. Among other American houses with rusticated façades that are still standing and were likely similarly painted are the Lee Mansion (1768) in Marblehead, Massachusetts; the Royal House (1747-50) in Medford, Massachusetts; and The Lindens (1754), originally built in Danvers, Massachusetts, and now reconstructed in Washington, D.C.

6. Downing and Scully, p. 454.

7. Ibid, pp. 94-95.

8. Pierson, p. 144.

Chapter 4

1. Abbott Lowell Cummings, conference address: "Paint in the American Colonies and Early Republic," Paint in America, A Symposium on Architectural and Decorative Paints, May 18, 1989.

2. Ibid.

3. William A. Flynt and Joseph Peter Spang, "Exterior Architectural Embellishment," *The Magazine Antiques* (March, 1985), p. 633.

4. Ibid.

5. The house has been recently repainted in this color scheme and can be visited at Deerfield. The original door surround is in the Henry Francis du Pont Winterthur Museum and that at the house is a reproduction.

6. For a photograph of this house and other authentically painted eighteenth-century residences, see "The Webb-Deane-Stevens Museum," *The Magazine Antiques* (March, 1976), pp. 534-541.

Chapter 5

1. Antoinette F. Downing and Vincent J. Scully, Jr., *The Architectural Heritage of Newport, Rhode Island* (New York: Bramhall House, 1967), p. 69.

2. Ibid.

3. William A. Flynt and Joseph Peter Spang, "Exterior Architectural Embellishment," *The Magazine Antiques* (March, 1985), p. 633.

4. Downing and Scully, p. 69.

5. Robert P. Emlen, "The Early Drawings of Elder Joshua Bussell," *The Magazine Antiques* (March, 1978), pp. 632-637.

6. Betty Ring, "Mary Balch's Newport Sampler," *The Magazine Antiques* (September, 1983), pp. 500-507.

7. Flynt and Spang, pp. 632-635.

Chapter 6

1. John W. Barber and Henry Howe, *Historical Collections of the State of New Jersey* (Newark, 1844), p. 286.

2. Ibid, p. 256.

Chapter 7

1. Richard M. Candee, "Preparing and Mixing Colors in 1812," *The Magazine Antiques* (April, 1978), pp. 849-853. This article includes photographs of each page of Reynolds's book.

2. Ibid, p. 852.

3. Jay E. Cantor, "The Landscape of Change, Views of Rural New England, 1790-1865," *The Magazine Antiques* (April, 1976), p. 779. The watercolors are in the collection of The Society for the Preservation of New-England Antiquities.

4. The whereabouts of Fitzhugh Lane's painting of a house in Castine, Maine, is unknown.

5. Diane Cox, "Gracie Mansion, Five Years and Six Million Later," *Historic Preservation* (April, 1985), pp. 21-25.

Chapter 8

1. Sarah Mytton Maury, *An Englishwoman in America* (Liverpool, 1848), pp. 163-164. A painting showing the house of Duncan Phyfe which was painted in this manner can be seen in an article by Elisabeth Donaghy Garrett, "The American Home," *The Magazine Antiques* (January, 1983), p. 222.

2. William H. Pierson, Jr., *American Buildings and Their Architects, The Colonial and Neoclassical Styles* (New York: Anchor Press / Doubleday, 1976), p. 253.

3. A reproduction of this painting can be seen in Marshall B. Davidson, *The American Heritage History of Notable American Houses* (New York: American Heritage Publishing Co., 1971), p. 145. The original painting is in the Museum of the City of New York.

4. A reproduction of this summertime view can be seen in Russell Bastedo, "American Paintings in the Long Island Historical Society," *The Magazine Antiques* (April, 1982), p. 926.

5. For a comprehensive study of the shutter in early America, see Elisabeth Donaghy Garrett, "The American Home; Part V: Venetian Shutters and Blinds," *The Magazine Antiques* (August, 1985), pp. 259-265.

6. A reproduction of this painting can be seen in Wendy Ann Cooper, "Paul Revere's Boston, 1735-1818," *The Magazine Antiques* (July, 1975), p. 87.

Chapter 9

1. William H. Pierson, Jr., *American Buildings and Their Architects, The Colonial and Neoclassical Styles* (New York: Anchor Press/Doubleday, 1976), p. 457. Pierson notes that this phenomenon was not uncommon in the South and gives Oak Alley (c. 1836) in St. James Parish, Louisiana, as an example.

2. Ibid, p. 453.

3. Ibid, pp. 455-456.

4. A Persac drawing of Hope Estate Plantation (c. 1857) at Baton Rouge, Louisiana, can be found in H. Parrott Bacot, "The Anglo-American Art Museum of Louisiana State University in Baton Rouge," *The Magazine Antiques* (March, 1984), p. 643.

5. For a color reproduction of Shadows-on-the-Teche drawn by Persac in 1861, see an article by William Nathaniel Banks, "Louisiana Plantations, the Bayou Country," *The Magazine Antiques* (July, 1984), p. 107.

6. For information on the restoration of the Henri Penne House, see an article by H. Parrott Bacot "The Henri Penne House Complex, Saint Martin Parish, Louisiana," *The Magazine Antiques* (April, 1988), pp. 906-913.

7. For a comprehensive study of the shutter in early America, see Elisabeth Donaghy Garrett, "The American Home; Part V: Venetian Shutters and Blinds," *The Magazine Antiques* (August, 1985), pp. 259-265.

8. For a house of similar style in another color scheme, see Jessie Poesch, "The Poydras-Holden House in Louisiana," *The Magazine Antiques* (April, 1985), pp. 870-877.

Chapter 10

1. A reproduction of this plate can be seen in William H. Pierson, Jr., *American Buildings and Their Architects, The Colonial and Neoclassical Styles* (New York: Anchor Press/Doubleday, 1976), p. 448.

2. William Seale, "Bulloch Hall in Roswell, Georgia," *The Magazine Antiques* (June, 1974), p. 1322.

3. For an example of a Greek Revival house with bright green shutters, see Jay E. Cantor, "The Landscape of Change, Views of Rural New England, 1790-1865," *The Magazine Antiques* (April, 1976), p. 780.

4. The builder of the Augustine House was very closely following Lafever's plate which indicated square pillars rather than round columns.

Chapter 11

1. Refer to the Introduction for information concerning Downing.

2. Fredrika Bremer, *The Homes of the New World: Impressions of America* (New York, 1853), p. 19.

3. The book was written as a travel journal by the Swedish diarist between 1849 and 1853.

4. Bremer, pp. 18-19.

5. For a comprehensive treatment of A. J. Downing refer to William H. Pierson, Jr., *American Buildings and Their Architects, The Colonial and Neoclassical Styles* (New York: Anchor Press/Doubleday, 1976), pp. 349-431.

6. William Nathaniel Banks, "Edgewater on the Hudson River," *The Magazine Antiques* (June, 1982), p. 1405.

7. Ibid.

8. Andrew Jackson Downing, *The Architecture of Country Houses* (New York: Dover Publications, 1969), p. 204.

Chapter 12

1. The wooden parapet has been conjecturally restored by the author.

2. Charles Lockwood, *Bricks and Brownstone, The New York Row House, 1783-1929, An Architectural and Social History* (New York: McGraw-Hill Book Company, 1972), p. 60.

3. Further research into this practice needs to be done. It may have some basis, however, in an eighteenth-century technique which involved painting the putty along window mullions black. As Frank S. Welsh, a noted historic paint researcher, has noted, this may have been done to make fat wooden mullions look thinner and the window glass larger. See *The Bulletin of the Association for Preservation Technology*, XII, no. 2 (1980), pp. 122-123.

Chapter 13

1. The two-paneled door is likely original to the house. The later-styled front door is an "upgrade" of the late nineteenth century.

2. Lewis F. Allen, *Rural Architecture* (New York, 1852), pp. ix-17.

3. Ibid, p. 42.

4. Ibid, p. 43.

5. Ibid, p. 44.

6. Ibid, p. 45.

7. One cannot help thinking of the architectural ideas of Frank Lloyd Wright (1867-1959) in relation to Downing and others.

8. The Lincoln House has been recently repainted according to its color scheme at the time it was owned by Lincoln.

9. Paintings steps in this fashion was a common procedure.

Chapter 14

1. Architectural styles translated to frontier regions have typically been characterized by a so-called "time lag."

2. Tavern signs generally depicted views and subjects other than buildings.

3. As noted by Roger Moss at "Paint in America," A Symposium on Architectural and Decorative Paints, May 18, 1989, green, because of its wide popularity, seems to have been the first ready-mixed paint in America, c. 1860s.

4. A contemporary painting showing the effects and use of the closed shutter can be seen in a painting by J. Russell of the parlor in the Abraham Russell House (c. 1848), New Bedford, Massachusetts. *The Magazine Antiques* (May, 1978), p. 1108.

5. For a comprehensive study of the use of the shutter in early America see Elisabeth Donaghy Garrett, "The American Home; Part V: Venetian Shutters and Blinds," *The Magazine Antiques* (August, 1985), pp. 259-265.

6. According to Theodore Zuk Penn in "Decorative and Protective Finishes, 1750-1850, Materials, Process and Craft," *The Bulletin of the Association for Preservation Technology,* XVI, no. 1 (1984), p. 15, the term "mineral green" was a name applied to green pigments of many types.

7. William A. Flynt and Joseph Peter Spang, "Exterior Architectural Embellishment," *The Magazine Antiques* (March, 1985), pp. 635-636. A photograph of the Williams house is on the cover of the issue.

8. Ibid.

Chapter 15

1. Sally B. Woodbridge and Roger Montgomery, *A Guide to Architecture in Washington State* (Seattle: University of Washington Press, 1980), p. 280.

2. Ibid, p. 282.

3. Constance M. Greiff, *Lost America: From the Mississippi to the Pacific* (Princeton: The Pyne Press, 1974), p. 36.

4. Ibid, p. 72.

5. Roger Sales, *Seattle Past to Present* (Seattle: University of Washington Press, 1976), p. 12.

Chapter 16

1. Information about Fowler's life and work can be found in Madeline B. Stern's introduction to *The Octagon House, A Home for All* by Orson Squire Fowler (New York: Dover Publications, 1973), pp. v-xii.

2. Ibid, p. vi.

3. Ibid.

4. John A. Garraty, *The American Nation, A History of the United States* (New York: American Heritage Publishing Co., 1966), pp. 352-353.

5. Ibid, p. 354.

6. Fowler, pp. vi, vii, 7-15.

7. Ibid, pp. 82-87.

8. Ibid, pp. x-xi.

9. Ibid, pp. 47-48.

10. Ibid, p. 48.

11. Ibid, pp. 7-15.

12. Andrew Jackson Downing, *The Architecture of Country Houses* (New York: Dover Publications, 1969), pp. 204-205.

13. Fowler, pp. 17-18.

14. Ibid, p. 48.

15. Elisabeth Donaghy Garrett, "The American Home; Part V: Venetian Shutters and Blinds," *The Magazine Antiques* (August, 1985), pp. 259-265.

Chapter 17

1. Carl W. Condit, *American Building, Materials and Techniques from the Beginning of the Colonial Settlements to the Present* (Chicago: University of Chicago Press, 1968), pp. 44-45.

2. "Winter Scene in New Haven, Connecticut," c. 1858; oil on canvas, 18 x 24 in., George Henry Durrie (1820-1863). National Museum of American Art.

3. Lewis F. Allen, *Rural Architecture* (New York, 1852), p. 47.

Chapter 18

1. Among the most popular writers during the period were such European romantics as Goethe, Byron, and Sir Walter Scott.

2. Wayne Andrews, *Architecture, Ambition, and Americans, A Social History of American Architecture* (New York: The Free Press, 1964), p. 106.

3. An introduction to the life and work of Andrew Jackson Downing can be found in an essay by George B. Tatum in *Master Builders, A Guide to Famous Architects,* ed. Diane Maddex (Washington, D.C.: The Preservation Press, 1985), pp. 60-63.

4. Andrew Jackson Downing, *Victorian Cottage Residences* (New York, Dover Publications, 1981), p. 116.

Chapter 19

1. Harold Kirker, *California's Architectural Frontier, Style and Tradition in the Nineteenth Century* (Salt Lake City: Peregrine Smith, 1986), pp. 32-33.

2. Ibid, pp. 34-35.

3. Charles Lockwood, *Suddenly San Francisco, The Early Years of an Instant City* (San Francisco: The San Francisco Examiner, 1978), pp. 19-20.

4. Ibid, p. 20.
5. Kirker, p. 42.
6. Ibid, pp. 62, 65.
7. Ibid, pp. 44-54.
8. A photograph of the Bowen House, painted according to this scheme, can be found in Roger W. Moss and Gail Caskey Winkler, *Victorian Exterior Decoration, How to Paint Your Nineteenth-Century American House Historically* (New York: Henry Holt and Co., 1987), p. 20.

Chapter 20

1. Harold Kirker, *California's Architectural Frontier, Style and Tradition in the Nineteenth Century* (Salt Lake City: Peregrine Smith, 1986), p. 47.
2. Specifications included in the HABS survey of Mosswood.
3. A color reproduction of these colors can be seen in Roger W. Moss and Gail Caskey Winkler, *Victorian Exterior Decoration, How To Paint Your Nineteenth-Century American House Historically* (New York: Henry Holt and Co., 1987), p. 18.
4. Lewis F. Allen, *Rural Architecture* (New York, 1852), p. 44.
5. Ibid.
6. A photograph of this house can be found in Moss and Winkler, p. 20.
7. Allen, p. 43.

Chapter 21

1. Refer to note 2, chapter 7 for modern paint equivalents.

Chapter 22

1. Refer to notes in chapter 7.
2. Advertisement, *The Magazine Antiques* (June, 1988).
3. Ibid.
4. For a color reproduction of a small Italianate villa designed by John Riddle, see John Maass, *The Victorian House in America* (New York: Hawthorn Books, 1972), plate IX.
5. Andrew Jackson Downing, *Victorian Cottage Residences* (New York: Dover Publications, 1981), p. 116.
6. We tend to forget the importance that both shutters and porches assumed during the last century in regulating heat and glare.

Chapter 23

1. In some cases, such as at the restored Gallier House in New Orleans, scoring lines were painted on exterior wall surfaces which had been colored in a stone-like fashion.

2. Apart from cost, many builders in the eighteenth-century were discouraged from using dressed stone because of a lack of available supplies.
3. *Philip Vickers Fithian, Journals and Letters (1773-1774)*, ed. Hunter Dickinson Farish (Williamsburg: Colonial Williamsburg, 1965), p. 80.
4. Andrew Jackson Downing, *Victorian Cottage Residences* (New York: Dover Publications, 1981), p. 8.
5. Andrew Jackson Downing, *The Architecture of Country Houses* (New York: Dover Publications, 1969), p. 64.
6. Ibid, p. 66.
7. Several contemporary paintings show green-painted iron porches.

Chapter 24

1. John C. Poppeliers, S. Allen Chambers, Jr., and Nancy B. Schwartz, *What Style Is It? A Guide to American Architecture* (Washington, D.C.: The Preservation Press, 1983), pp. 46-49, 52-55.
2. Andrew Jackson Downing, *Victorian Cottage Residences* (New York: Dover Publications, 1981), p. 14.
3. A color photograph of this painting can be seen in John Maass, *The Victorian Home in America* (New York: Hawthorn Books, 1972), plate VIII.
4. Ibid, p. 168.
5. Daniel T. Atwood, *Atwood's Country and Suburban Houses* (New York, 1871), p. 238.

Chapter 25

1. Information about professional builders and architects in early California can be found in Harold Kirker, *California's Architectural Frontier, Style and Tradition in the Nineteenth Century* (Salt Lake City: Peregrine Smith, 1986), pp. 23-54.
2. A reproduction of the six colors suggested by Downing in *Cottage Residences* (1842) can be found in Roger W. Moss and Gail Caskey Winkler, *Victorian Exterior Decoration, How to Paint Your Nineteenth-Century American House Historically* (New York: Henry Holt and Co., 1987), p. 18. Modern commercially available paints corresponding to these colors might include the following: Gray A, Somerset Gray (Cook and Dunn); Gray B, Tankard No. 417631 (Glidden); Gray C, Breton Blue (California Paints/Newport); Fawn D, Alamo Stone, No. 3480 (Pittsburgh); Fawn E,. Ballroom Tan, No. 21 GV-P (Pratt and Lambert); Fawn F, Golden Maple, No. 4492 (Pittsburgh).

Chapter 26

1. An excellent discussion of this house can be found in the introduction to Vincent J. Scully, Jr., *The Shingle Style and The Stick Style, Architectural Theory and Design from Downing to the Origins of Wright* (New Haven: Yale University Press, 1972).

2. Andrew Jackson Downing, *Victorian Cottage Residences* (New York: Dover Publications, 1981), p. 10.

3. Sarah Bradford Landau, "Richard Morris Hunt: Architectural Innovator and Father of a"Distinctive' American School," in *The Architecture of Richard Morris Hunt,* ed. Susan P. Stein (Chicago: The University of Chicago Press, 1986), p. 52. This essay also includes interesting early photographs of the Griswold House and similar houses.

4. Andrew Jackson Downing, *The Architecture of Country Houses* (New York: Dover Publications, 1969), pp. 127-128.

5. Ibid, pp. 50-53, 127-128.

6. Landau, pp. 52-53.

7. Ibid, p. 53.

8. Ibid, pp. 52-53.

9. Care must be taken in "reading" color from black and white nineteenth-century photographs. Ascertaining definite colors or shades of color from them is of course impossible, although noting the contrast of light and dark tones in such photographs can be helpful in planning color schemes.

10. Susan R. Stein, "Role and Reputation: The Architectural Practice of Richard Morris Hunt," in *The Architecture of Richard Morris Hunt,* ed. Susan R. Stein (Chicago: The University of Chicago Press, 1986), p. 113.

11. Landau, p. 49.

12. Ibid, p. 51.

Chapter 27

1. David G. McCullough, "Oak Bluffs," *American Heritage* (October, 1967), p. 39. This article is illustrated with excellent contemporary photographs of several cottages.

2. Ibid, p. 38. One of the photographs shows a placard above a front door, reading "In the first glass Lies the Sin."

3. Ibid.

4. Examples of this color's popularity can be seen in Roger W. Moss and Gail Caskey Winkler, *Victorian Exterior Decoration, How to Paint Your Nineteenth-Century American House Historically* (New York: Henry Holt and Co., 1987), pp. 14, 71, 90.

Chapter 28

1. John C. Poppeliers, S. Allen Chambers, Jr., and Nancy B. Schwartz, *What Style Is It? A Guide to American Architecture* (Washington, D.C.: The Preservation Press, 1983), pp. 56-61.

2. Photographs of the period often show "high-style" houses painted in what appears to be white with little, if any, color embellishment except for dark painted window sash and doors. One example can be seen in John Maas, *The Victorian Home in America* (New York: Hawthorn Books, 1972), p. 131.

3. Ibid, plate XII.

4. See note 9, chapter 26.

Chapter 29

1. John C. Poppeliers, S. Allen Chambers, Jr., and Nancy B. Schwartz, *What Style Is It? A Guide to American Architecture* (Washington, D.C.: The Preservation Press, 1983), p. 57.

2. Naming eclectic architectural styles has never been an easy task.

3. A good picture essay of Queen Anne-style houses can be found in Arnold Lewis, *American Country Houses of the Gilded Age (from Sheldon's "Artistic Country-Seats")* (New York: Dover Publications, 1982).

4. Lewis Mumford, *The Brown Decades, A Study of the Arts in America, 1865-1895* (New York: Dover Publications, 1955), pp. 4-9.

5. Excellent period color plates and commentary about color placement in Victorian houses can be found in Roger W. Moss and Gail Caskey Winkler, *Victorian Exterior Decoration, How to Paint Your Nineteenth-Century American House Historically* (New York: Henry Holt and Co., 1987).

6. The Haas-Lilienthal House in San Francisco has been painted in an historically accurate combination of grays.

Chapter 30

1. An example of colored mortar joints can be seen on Sagamore Hill, Theodore Roosevelt's house, Oyster Bay, Long Island, New York. The house and grounds are open to the public.

2. One theory about the maintenance of this trim color is that dark green is easier to cover with dark green than with white. In several instances it seems as if repainting trimwork—one of the most tedious of jobs—was done in the easiest of manners.

3. One building recently restored to this painted treatment is the Longstreet Library at the Peddie School, Hightstown, New Jersey (c. 1887).

Chapter 31

1. See chapter 30, The Middlecoff-Baier House.

Chapter 32

1. One of the most comprehensive studies of the development of the Colonial Revival style can be found in Vincent J. Scully, Jr., *The Shingle Style and the Stick Style, Architectural Theory and Design from Downing to the Origins of Wright.* (New Haven: Yale University Press, 1955), pp. 19 ff.

2. Leland M. Roth, *McKim, Mead and White, Architects* (New York: Harper and Row, 1985), p. 96.

3. Scully, plate 149.

Chapter 33

1. Folke Nyberg and Victor Steinbrueck, consultants, *An Urban Inventory for Seattle; Wallingford: An Inventory of Buildings and Urban Design Resources* (Seattle: Historic Seattle Preservation and Development Authority, 1975), "a note on the Wallingford Bungalow."

2. Orson S. Fowler, *The Octagon House, A Home for All* (New York: Dover Publications, 1973), pp. 82-87.

3. Gustav Stickley, *The Best of Craftsman Homes* (Santa Barbara and Salt Lake City: Peregrine Smith, 1979), pp. 6-9.

4. John C. Poppeliers, S. Allen Chambers, Jr., and Nancy B. Schwartz, *What Style Is It? A Guide to American Architecture* (Washington, D.C.: The Preservation Press, 1983), pp. 76-79.

5. An introduction to the life and work of Julia Morgan can be found in an essay by Sara Holmes Boutelle in *Master Builders, A Guide to Famous American Architects,* ed. Diane Maddex (Washington, D.C.: The Preservation Press, 1985), pp. 132-135.

6. Sara Holmes Boutelle, *Julia Morgan, Architect* (New York: Abbeville Press, 1988), p. 122.

7. The garden walls at the Robson-Harrington Park in San Anselmo, California, date from this period and are excellent examples of the rich textural materials favored at this time.

8. Strickley, p. 64.

Chapter 34

1. Historic American Buildings Survey information.

2. Many of these labels have been coined by real estate agents to describe buildings more precisely.

3. A good essay on the work and influence of Stickley is Barry Sanders' introduction to *The Best of Craftsman Homes* (Santa Barbara and Salt Lake City: Peregrine Smith, 1979).

4. Ibid, pp. 12-14.

5. Ibid, p. 14.

6. Ibid, p. 134.

7. Ibid, p. 20.

Chapter 35

1. John C. Poppeliers, S. Allen Chambers, Jr., and Nancy B. Schwartz, *What Style Is It? A Guide to American Architecture* (Washington, D.C.: The Preservation Press, 1983), pp. 80-83.

2. Ibid, pp. 84-85.

3. See note 3, chapter 34.

4. Ibid, pp. 12-14.

5. Ibid, p. 20. In this instance, the soft gray was chosen to harmonize with the house's fieldstone base and the shingled roof was painted a "soft moss green."

6. Ibid, pp. 76-77.

Bibliography

Books

Andrews, Wayne. *Architecture, Ambition and Americans.* New York: The Free Press, 1964.

Atwood, Daniel T. *Atwood's Country and Suburban Homes.* New York: Orange Judd and Co., 1871.

Barber, John W. and Henry Howe. *Historical Collections of the State of New Jersey.* Newark: Benjamin Olds, 1844.

Bouetelle, Sara Holmes. *Julia Morgan, Architect.* New York: Abbeville Press, 1988.

Bremer, Frederika. *The Homes of the New World, Impressions of America.* 2 vols. New York: Harper and Bros., 1853.

Condit, Carl W. *American Buildings, Materials and Techniques from the Beginning of the Colonial Settlements to the Present.* Chicago: University of Chicago Press, 1968.

Davidson, Marshall B. *The American Heritage History of Notable American Houses.* New York: American Heritage Publishing Co., 1971.

Dickinson, Hunter, ed. *Philip Vickers Fithian, Journals and Letters, 1773-1774.* Williamsburg: Colonial Williamsburg, 1965.

Downing, Andrew Jackson. *The Architecture of Country Houses.* New York: Dover Publications, 1969.

_____ . *Victorian Cottage Residences.* New York: Dover Publications, 1981.

Downing, Antoinette and Vincent J. Scully, Jr. *The Architectural Heritage of Newport, Rhode Island.* New York: Bramhall House, 1967.

Fowler, Orson Squire. *The Octagon House, A Home for All.* New York: Dover Publications, 1973.

Garraty, John A. *The American Nation, A History of the United States.* New York: American Heritage Publishing Co., 1966.

Gowans, Alan. *Images of American Living, Four Centuries of Architecture and Furniture as Cultural Expression.* Philadelphia: J.B. Lippincott Co., 1964.

Greiff, Constance M. *Lost America, From the Mississippi to the Pacific.* Princeton: The Pyne Press, 1974.

Kirker, Harold. *California's Architectural Frontier, Style and Tradition in the Nineteenth Century.* Salt Lake City: Peregrine Smith, 1986.

Lewis, Arnold. *American Country Houses of the Gilden Age.* New York: Dover Publications, 1982.

Lockwood, Charles. *Bricks and Brownstone, The New York Row House, 1783-1929, An Architectural and Social History.* New York: McGraw-Hill, 1972.

_____ . *Suddenly San Francisco, The Early Years of an Instant City.* San Francisco: San Francisco Examiner, 1978.

Maas, John. *The Victorian Home in America.* New York: Hawthorn Books, 1972.

Maddex, Diane, ed. *Master Builders, Guide to Famous American Architects.* Washington, D.C.: The Preservation Press, 1985.

Morrison, Hugh. *Early American Architecture, From the First Colonial Settlements to the National Period.* New York: Oxford University Press, 1952.

Moss, Roger W. and Gail Caskey Winkler. *Victorian Exterior Decoration, How to Paint Your Nineteenth-Century American House Historically.* New York: Henry Holt and Co., 1987.

Mumford, Lewis. *The Brown Decades, A Study of the Arts in America, 1865-1895.* New York: Dover Publications, 1955.

Nyberg, Folke and Victor Steinbrueck, eds. *A Visual Inventory of Buildings and Urban Design Resources for Seattle, Washington.* Seattle: Historic Seattle Preservation and Development Authority, 1975.

Pierson, William H., Jr. *American Buildings and Their Architects, Technology and the Picturesque, The Corporate and the Early Gothic Styles.* Garden City, N.Y.: Doubleday and Co., 1978.

_____ . *American Buildings and Their Architects, The Colonial and Neoclassical Styles.* New York: Anchor Press/Doubleday, 1976.

Poppeliers, John C., S. Allen Chambers, Jr., and Nancy B. Schwartz. *What Style Is It? A Guide to American Architecture.* Washington, D.C.: The Preservation Press, 1983.

Reynolds, Hezekiah. *Directions for House and Ship Painting.* New Haven, 1812. (A facsimile of this book has been reproduced in Richard M. Candee, "Preparing and Mixing Colors in 1812," *The Magazine Antiques,* April, 1978, pp. 849-853).

Roth, Leland M. *McKim, Mead and White, Architects.* New York: Harper & Row, 1983.

Scully, Vincent J., Jr. *The Shingle Style and the Stick Style, Architectural Theory and Design from Downing to the Origins of Wright.* New Haven: Yale University Press, 1973.

Stein, Susan R., ed. *The Architecture of Richard Morris Hunt.* Chicago: University of Chicago Press, 1986.

Stickley, Gustav. *The Best of Craftsman Homes.* Santa Barbara and Salt Lake City: Peregrine Smith, 1979.

Whiffen, Marcus. *The Eighteenth-Century Houses of Williamsburg, A Study of Architecture and Building in the Colonial Capital of Virginia.* Williamsburg: Colonial Williamsburg, 1960.

Woodbridge, Sally B. *California Architecture, Historic American Buildings Survey.* San Francisco: Chronicle Books, 1988.

Woodbridge, Sally B. and Roger Montgomery. *A Guide to Architecture in Washington State.* Seattle: University of Washington Press, 1980.

Articles

Alderson, Caroline. "Recreating a Nineteenth-Century Paint Palette." *The Bulletin of the Association for Preservation Technology,* vol. XVI, no. 1 (1984), pp. 47-56.

Banks, William Nathaniel. "Edgewater on the Hudson River." *The Magazine Antiques* (June, 1982), pp. 1400-1410.

Bacot, H. Parrott. "The Henri Penne House Complex, Saint Martin Parish, Louisiana." *The Magazine Antiques* (April, 1986), pp. 906-913.

Blackburn, Roderic H. "Dutch Arts and Culture in Colonial America." *The Magazine Antiques* (July, 1986), pp. 140-151.

Candee, Richard M. "Preparing and Mixing Colors in 1812." *The Magazine Antiques* (April, 1978), pp. 849-853.

Cantor, Jay E. "The Landscape of Change, Views of Rural New England, 1790-1865." *The Magazine Antiques* (April, 1976), pp. 772-783.

Emlen, Robert P. "The Early Drawings of Elder Joshua Bussell." *The Magazine Antiques* (March, 1978), pp. 632-637.

Flynt, William A. and Joseph Peter Spang. "Exterior Architectural Embellishment." *The Magazine Antiques* (March, 1985), pp. 632-639.

Garrett, Elisabeth Donaghy. "The American Home, Part V: Venetian Shutters and Blinds." *The Magazine Antiques* (August, 1985), pp. 870-877.

McCullough, David G. "Oak Bluffs." *American Heritage,* vol. XVIII, no. 6 (October, 1967), pp. 38-47.

Mosca, Matthew John. "The House and Its Restoration." *The Magazine Antiques* (February, 1989), pp. 462-473.

Penn, Theodore Zuk. "Decorative and Protective Finishes, 1750-1850, Materials, Process and Craft." *The Bulletin of the Association for Preservation Technology,* vol. XVI, no. 1 (1984), pp. 3-45.

Ring, Betty. "Mary Balch's Newport Sampler." *The Magazine Antiques* (September, 1983), pp. 500-507.

Seale, William. "Bulloch Hall in Roswell, Georgia." *The Magazine Antiques* (June, 1974), pp. 1322-1329.

Watkins, Susan Finlay. "The Webb-Deane-Stevens Museum." *The Magazine Antiques* (March, 1976), pp. 534-541.

Welsh, Frank S. "18th Century Black Window Glazing in Philadelphia." *The Bulletin of the Association for Preservation Technology,* vol. XII, no. 2 (1980), pp. 122-123.

Index